*James Salter*

Twayne's United States Authors Series

Frank Day, Editor
*Clemson University*

TUSAS 707

JAMES SALTER
*Courtesy of James Salter*

# *James Salter*

## William Dowie

*Southeastern Louisiana University*

**Twayne Publishers**
An Imprint of Simon & Schuster Macmillan
New York

**Prentice Hall International**
London • Mexico City • New Delhi • Singapore • Sydney • Toronto

Twayne's United States Author Series No. 707

*James Salter*
William Dowie

Twayne Publishers
An Imprint of Simon & Schuster Macmillan
1633 Broadway
New York, NY 10019

**Library of Congress Cataloging-in-Publication Data**

Dowie, William, 1940–
    James Salter / William Dowie.
      p.  cm. — (Twayne's United States authors series ; TUSAS 707)
    Includes bibliographical references (p.   ) and index.
    ISBN 0-8057-1604-1 (alk. paper)
    1. Salter, James—Criticism and interpretation.   I. Title.
    II. Series.
    PS3569.A4622Z64    1998
    813'.54—dc21
                                    98-27006
                                        CIP

PS
3569
.A1622
Z64
1998

10 9 8 7 6 5 4 3 2 1

Printed in the United States of America

AGO1581

*A garland of gratitude on the gravestone of my parents,*
*William J. Dowie Sr. (1909–1959)*
*and*
*Ruth Kent Dowie (1909–1967)*

# Contents

# Preface

"The favor of all the novel writers in the world," wrote William Dean Howells, "could not solely make a novel successful; and yet if the novelists liked it I should say it was surely a good novel."[1] Howells knew first-hand the inconsequentiality of peer adulation on popular success. Both he and his eminent contemporary Henry James published to the applause of their fellow novelists and the indifference of the public. The popular novelists of their day were Marie Corelli, Ian Maclaren, Anthony Hope, and F. Hopkinson Smith, all long since buried in the graveyard of forgotten authors. Meanwhile Howells and James have been reincarnated as golden birds of the literary aviary, nesting in every respectable bookstore in the country and exhibited before successive generations of students. They continue to sing "to lords and ladies of Byzantium / Of what is past, or passing, or to come."[2] Unquestionably this transformation depended, to some extent, on the response of a third component of the reading audience, the academy, as it accorded their novels the esteem of critical scrutiny. Ultimately, then, success depends on all three estates of the reading audience: peers, public, and academy—each exerting its peculiar influence on the other two.

One wonders how many novelists writing today have earned the respect of their fellow writers, only to have their books collect more dust than fingerprints. We in the academy usually hear of such only after they have made a public splash or a sympathetic school of criticism has adopted them. William Kennedy was such an unknown, admired in small literary circles exclusively, until Saul Bellow persuaded Viking to publish *Ironweed* after its editorial board had already rejected the book. The cards then all fell in line: an enterprising editor hit on a unique marketing approach, and the book became a best-seller and won the Pulitzer Prize. Anne Tyler had published eight novels and was simply a writer's writer before her *Dinner at the Homesick Restaurant* got a rave review on the front page of the *New York Times Book Review.* Her next novel enjoyed equal acclaim and popularity, and her early books were reprinted and widely distributed. Each successive book has made the best-seller lists. This so-called breakout phenomenon, as described by Joseph Barbato in his *Publishers Weekly* article, was exemplified most dramatically when John Irving's *The World According to Garp* appeared in

1978.[3] Irving's three previous novels, published by Random House, had successively smaller sales, the last of these selling fewer than 3,000 copies. When he wrote *Garp,* his editor, Joe Fox, liked the book but, because of dwindling enthusiasm at Random House, suggested that Irving take it to another publisher. He did, and the book swept the imagination of the country, casting every Irving offering thereafter into the warm spotlight of public attention. Of course, no contemporary author had labored more faithfully in obscurity, or with greater artistic integrity, than Cormac McCarthy, until *All the Pretty Horses* (1992) won the National Book Award and caught the fancy of the reading public. Sometimes attention is focused on a deserving writer by other media, as in the case of Ernest Gaines, whose *The Autobiography of Miss Jane Pittman* became one of the most watched miniseries in television history. Recently Gaines received another boost when he was featured on the *Oprah Winfrey Show*, vaulting his novel *A Lesson before Dying* to the top of the 1997 paperback best-seller lists despite the fact it was initially published in 1993. These are all worthy writers, whose success is well deserved. Yet given the vagaries of fortune, there are equally, perhaps more, worthy writers who have not yet basked in the warm glow of public appreciation. Among the ranks of the underappreciated are Vance Bourjaily, John Ehle, James Wilcox, and James Salter. A case could be made for each of these writers, but it is Salter who most exactly fits both halves of Howells's dictum, a perfect illustration of peer favor and public disinterest.

Salter's writing career did not begin until he was 31 with the publication of a novel, *The Hunters* (1956), followed by another, *The Arm of Flesh* (1961). Not until he was 41 did he produce a work of consequence, the novel *A Sport and a Pastime* (1967). Since then he has written two other novels, *Light Years* (1975) and *Solo Faces* (1979), a collection of short stories, *Dusk and Other Stories* (1988), and a memoir, *Burning the Days* (1997).

In 1984 *Esquire* said that Salter "has been more appreciated by more serious literary authors than has any other modern American writer."[4] The list of Salter's literary advocates surely bears out this superlative. Saul Bellow, Graham Greene, Irwin Shaw, Mavis Gallant, Reynolds Price, Glenway Wescott, Joy Williams, John Irving, Joseph Heller, Richard Ford, and Michael Ondaatje have all praised Salter's fiction enthusiastically. Price said Salter's *A Sport and a Pastime* is "as nearly perfect as any American fiction I know."[5] Bellow lauded Salter as "exceptionally talented," adding that such talent "turns me around, gives me new bearings, changes my views somewhat."[6] Joy Williams hailed *Light Years* as "an absolutely beautiful, monstrous, important book, one that I can simply not remove from my mind or my life."[7] Playwright A. R. Gurney called Salter "a long underestimated American writer" who is "worth more attention than he has received so far."[8] And Mavis Gallant described him as "a marvel," who "knows an uncanny amount about women."[9]

Salter received the P.E.N./Faulkner Award in 1992. His short stories have been selected for the O. Henry collections of *Prize Stories* in 1970, 1972, 1974, and 1984; for *The Best American Short Stories* in 1984; and for *American Short Story Masterpieces* in 1987. The Modern Library added *A Sport and a Pastime* to its list of distinguished classics in 1995. His five novels have received mostly favorable reviews. His collection, *Dusk and Other Stories,* was praised enthusiastically by reviewers, as was his recent memoir, *Burning the Days.* James Wolcott, writing in *Vanity Fair,* dubbed Salter "the most underrated underrated writer . . . whose best novels are . . . all brilliant."[10] And Susan Sontag ranks him "among the very few North American writers all of whose work I want to read, whose as yet unpublished books I wait for impatiently."[11]

And yet all of this praise, as Howells had foreseen, has not led to what the world calls success. Salter's novels have not sold well, *Solo Faces* being his top seller at about 12,000 copies. All five novels had dropped out of print until North Point Press issued new editions of *A Sport and a Pastime* and *Light Years.* Twenty years after the book's original publication, Vintage reissued *Light Years* in a trade paperback. And Counterpoint brought out a new hardcover edition, with revisions, of *The Hunters* in 1997. *Burning the Days,* which both publisher and author promoted with more than the accustomed publicity, has sold 22,500 copies in six months, not bad but far short of the sales of other personal memoirs in the 1990s.

Salter's lack of success, moreover, extends beyond the realm of mass popularity. The academy has been as indifferent as the masses. Since the time of his first novel in 1956 to the present, only three entries on Salter have appeared in the MLA annual bibliography, two of them in 1982. The first referenced a fine attempt by Margaret Winchell Miller in the *Hollins Critic* to introduce Salter to the academic community.[12] The second noted my essay in Armand Singer's *Essays on the Literature of Mountaineering* (1982), which argued that *Solo Faces* is not only head and shoulders above the mass of mountain fiction but fits squarely and honorably within the American literary tradition.[13] And the last indexed my

interpretation of his major novels in *College English.*[14] Beyond these, the
only recognition of Salter in the academic community was Harold
Bloom's listing of *Solo Faces* and *Light Years* in *The Western Canon* (1994)
as among the most important books of the twentieth century. Otherwise, the academy has ignored Salter. No mention of him was made in
James Vinson's *Contemporary Novelists* (1982), which featured sketches of
more than 600 writers. Nothing about Salter appeared in books about
contemporary American literature such as Joseph Epstein's *Plausible
Prejudices: Essays on American Writing* (1985) or Daniel Hoffman's *Har-
vard Guide to Contemporary American Literature* (1979). Even Frederick
Karl's *American Fictions, 1940–1980: A Comprehensive History and Critical
Evaluation* (1983) overlooked Salter completely, despite its pretentious
subtitle. More recent surveys, such as *The Columbia History of the American Novel* (1991) and *A Reader's Guide to the Twentieth Century Novel*
(1995), perpetuate the omission of Salter.

Why the critical neglect? Is Salter destined to remain strictly a writer's
writer? Will he continue to be read by subscribers to *Esquire,* the *Paris
Review,* and *Grand Street* in the same fashion that an actress in his story
"The Cinema" reads the lines of her part: "They were like shoes. She tried
them on, they were nice, she never thought who had made them."[15]

A portrait of a novelist in one of Salter's stories, "Via Negativa,"
modeled on a writer he knew who early in life published two stories in
*Esquire* but nothing more, bears more than a little resemblance to Salter
himself or to any writer who plugs along without fame:

> There is a kind of minor writer who is found in a room of the library sign-
> ing his novel. His index finger is the color of tea, his smile filled with bad
> teeth. He knows literature, however. His sad bones are made of it. He
> knows what was written and where writers died. His opinions are cold
> but accurate. They are pure, at least there is that.
>     He's unknown, though not without a few admirers. They are really
> like marriage, uninteresting, but what else is there? His life is his journals.
> In them somewhere is a line from the astrologer: your natural companions
> are women. Occasionally, perhaps. No more than that. His hair is thin.
> His clothes are a little out of style. He is aware, however, that there is a
> great, a final glory which falls on certain figures barely noticed in their
> time, touches them in obscurity and recreates their lives. His heroes are
> Musil and, of course, Gerard Manley Hopkins. Bunin. (*D,* 120)

Although the shabby appearance does not fit Salter, photographs often
show him with a wistful, even sad, expression. Other features like the

opinions and companions match, and he knows what was written and where writers are buried, having visited the graves of Keats, Robert Southey, Willa Cather, Swift, and Pirandello, to name only a few. In fact, when I first met Salter in July of 1985 in Sag Harbor, where he was living in a rented house while building a home in nearby Bridgehampton, foremost on his guided local tour was a stop at the cemetery where James Jones was buried. We also paid our respects at the Monument to Masters, a moving tribute in stone to the generations who hunted the great whales. In the course of the day, we spoke of the glory that comes from great deeds and great books, and of the necessity of taking the long view. Salter is fully aware of himself as sitting in the anteroom of fame, patiently waiting to be called. He believes in himself and the quality of his work, but he also believes there is no greatness without recognition. In life or after death, one must be read widely to qualify. And that has not yet happened.

I imagine the process of determining which writers will last, like James and even Howells, and which will be forgotten, like Marie Corelli and even Hamilton Basso, occurring in a giant colander filled with all books ever written. Some books, despite initial impressions, prove too thin and insubstantial; they slip through the colander's holes and are gone as soon as they are tossed about. They are not missed, and their authors are reduced to footnotes. Some books keep rising to the top after repeated shakings and many rotations past the gaps; such are unmistakable and remarkable, and their authors, despite periods of neglect, are acclaimed by their peers, the professors, and the reading public. Still other books survive the apertures but rarely surface, by chance remaining hidden in the mix except for infrequent sightings and occasional testimonials. Their authors' names become secrets, known only to the watchful and the fortunate or to fellow authors whose books theirs have brushed. For this group there is hope but no assurance. Their work has merit, but only time will tell if it is the kind that lasts.

Salter belongs to this last group. Although his admirers are more numerous than those of the minor writer in his story, "his reputation," as one reviewer notes, "is of a curious kind; no single book of his has a secure place in the canon of modern fiction. As a writer he is both known and not known."[16] His first two books, thin initial experiments, have almost slipped through the colander's openings, although renewed interest in *The Hunters* has sparked a revised hardcover edition. His other works, despite failing to reach a wide readership, show evidence of durability and substance. Witnesses with literary credibility testify not only

that his three major novels and a handful of his stories have survived the
colander's shuffles up until now but that his name will one day glow in
the pantheon.

What they say about Salter's writing is that it is lyrical and canny,
that his best work will take your breath away with sudden glimpses
deep into the pool of life. Indeed it is hard to read a Salter story without
being ambushed by recognitions, things one knew instinctively but
never thought about or acted on. Such a flash occurs regarding the
nature of commitments in the story "Lost Sons" as the narrator discovers
his past at a West Point reunion: "The haze of June lay over the great
expanse that separated him from those endless tasks of years before.
How deeply he had immersed himself in them. How ardently he had
believed in the image of a soldier. He had known it as a faith, he had
clung to it dumbly, as a cripple clings to God" (D, 98). Salter believes in
the power of language to move, and he stakes much of his fictional gamble on such brief passages. In the novel *Light Years* he writes about a
woman who is reading a book: "The power to change one's life comes
from a paragraph, a lone remark. The lines that penetrate us are slender,
like the flukes that live in river water and enter the bodies of swimmers."[17] This passage could stand as Salter's credo. He constantly strives
for such illuminations, usually the effect of a closing sentence that crystallizes what has gone before. His admirers swear, with the solemnity of
a secret oath, to his success. And yet, now in the twilight of his career at
73, he still awaits not only that "final glory which falls on certain figures" but even the standard recognition befitting a worthy and unique
voice in American fiction.

Irwin Shaw, Salter's friend and father figure, once told the younger
writer that the difference between them lay in Salter's being a lyrical,
while Shaw was a narrative, writer. Salter recalls that " 'lyric' seemed a
word [Shaw] was uncomfortable with. It seemed to mean something
like callow."[18] Indeed there is nothing callow about Salter's lyricism,
although it does stem from his boyhood attraction to poetry, the genre
of his maiden literary voyages in high school. When he turned to fiction
as an adult, Salter continued to draw inspiration from poets like John
Berryman, Lorca, Philip Larkin, and Pound, with particular admiration
for the *Cantos*. In his *Paris Review* interview, Salter admits a similarity
between the *Cantos* and some of his novels in the way they are built
around central luminous moments.[19]

The modernist movement pioneered by Pound, Hemingway, Fitzgerald, and Faulkner—with its blurring of genres and its creation of the

lyrical novel—laid the groundwork for the kind of fiction Salter would
write. Although his debt to Hemingway is clouded by Salter's avowed
scorn for Hemingway's character, Salter's style owes much to Hemingway's "word-by-word approach to writing through which he sought to
endow prose with the density of poetry, making each image, each scene,
each rendered act serve several purposes."[20] When asked about favorite
writers, Salter is quick to name Isaac Babel, who "has the three essen-
tials of greatness: style, structure and authority." But he goes on to
admit that "Hemingway, in fact, had those three things. But Babel particularly appeals to me because of the added element of his life, which
seems to me to give his work an additional poignancy" ("Art," 86). In
other words, writers' lives matter to Salter, especially when they mani-
fest heroism or magnanimity, for he says, "My idea of writing is of
unflinching and continual effort, somehow trying to find the right
words until you reach a point where you can make no further progress
and you either have something or you don't" ("Art," 86). His words echo
Hemingway, who did much to promote the public image of the writer as
hero. Hemingway's authenticity, however, is canceled for Salter by his
shoddy treatment of other writers who had befriended him like Sherwood Anderson and Ford Madox Ford.

   Yet it is Hemingway's type of novel that Salter wrote when he
penned his masterpiece, *A Sport and a Pastime,* for that book was made
possible by *The Sun Also Rises,* which set the pattern for "craft driving
fragmentary scenes and provocative characters before it" (Wagner-
Martin, 877). Both novels also feature triadic relationships and expatri-
ate Americans frustrated by desire. Salter had already tried and failed at
Faulkner with his previous novel, *The Arm of Flesh,* which attempted the
same multiple narrative technique of *As I Lay Dying* with disastrous
effect. It served as an apprenticeship, however, and Salter admits that
when he went on to his next book, *A Sport and a Pastime,* he was still
"under the spell of books which were brief but every page of which was
exalted, Faulkner's *The Sound and the Fury* or *As I Lay Dying.* This sort of
book, like those of Flannery O'Connor, Marguerite Duras, Camus,
remains my favorite. It is like the middle distances for a runner. The
pace is unforgiving and must be kept up to the end. The Finns were
once renowned for running these distances and the quality that was
demanded was *sisu,* courage and endurance. For me the shorter novels
show it best" (*BD,* 316–17).

   In other words, Salter will never write an *Anna Karenina* or a *Brothers
Karamazov,* and he will never exhibit the narrative panoramas of John

Irving, Don DeLillo, or Saul Bellow. If there is anything that will limit his reputation, that will allow his work to slip through the colander's openings, it is this relative lack of narrative scope. Somehow, such a lack did not hinder Hemingway and Fitzgerald, who created the right resonances for their lyrical masterpieces, *The Sun Also Rises* and *The Great Gatsby,* to become emblems of their time. Perhaps Salter's novel of desire and travel, *A Sport and a Pastime,* will come to represent the 1960s, a decade of exploration and liberation, in the same fashion that Hemingway's and Fitzgerald's books expressed the 1920s. *Light Years,* a novel of domesticity and divorce, might be the fresco that captures the dissolution of family life so roundly observed in the 1970s. *Solo Faces* could well come to epitomize the rush to challenge all physical limitations in the theater of the outdoors that has typified the last two decades. And Salter's latest offering, *Burning the Days,* a memoir whose many stories touch on all the great events of the last 75 years, could be seen by later generations as a tapestry of our century. Of course, the ultimate measure of literary achievement cannot be reduced to a work's success at embodying and capturing a period in history. There are other dimensions, not the least of which is the universal. But then, some things must be left for the rest of the book.

On 13 June 1983, James Salter wrote a short note to me after coming across my article on his novel *Solo Faces.* He said he "particularly liked" my description of my own climbing endeavors as "rather limited." Little did he know just how limited they were. We have corresponded on and off since then. Our first meeting was in the summer of 1985 in Sag Harbor. In the spring of 1989, I spent a weekend with him at the University of Alabama, where he was at the end of a two-week artist-in-residenceship. And in January 1997, I interviewed him for the greater part of two afternoons, the first in the coffee shop of the Guggenheim Museum and the second in the lounge of the Algonquin Hotel. His generosity and frankness in answering my questions have been invaluable in writing this book, whose errors I own completely.

# *Acknowledgments*

The person who told me to read James Salter was Rob Taylor, and that, as they say, has made all the difference. My ideas about Salter's writing have been refined by the reactions of others, particularly James Raymond, former editor of *College English,* and Frank Day, the general editor of this series. Salter himself has helped me understand his work by generously commenting on his intentions, influences, and life.

I am particularly indebted to Southeastern Louisiana University and its president, Dr. Sally Clausen; my dean, Dr. John Miller; and my department head, Dr. Sue Parrill, for the sabbatical that allowed me to write this book. Such support is exemplary and generative. When I needed to talk about the final stages of the labor, my colleague Dr. Carole McAllister listened patiently and advised sagely. I must also include my students in this thanks, for their enthusiasm has given me hope; one of them, Nicole dos Ramos, read the manuscript and offered timely suggestions.

It was Professor Armand Singer who first accepted my ideas about a Salter novel in his *Essays on the Literature of Mountaineering* (Morgantown: West Virginia University Press, 1982). I am grateful to him as well for allowing me to base chapter 6 on that essay. Likewise, parts of my article in *College English* (January 1989) are spread throughout the book. And I have used passages from my entry on Salter in the *Dictionary of Literary Biography*'s volume 130, *American Short Story Writers Since World War II,* edited by Patrick Meanor (Detroit: Gale, 1993), in chapter 7.

Writing a book is never easy on those closest to you, but Alba made it look easy. The rest of my family, Chris and Michael, Jan and Mark, Deb and Rob, have all helped by their encouragement and by ensuring that my cabin remain a hallowed place. And what could have been better than being near Cameron in the first year of his life?

# Chronology

1967–1969   Takes family abroad to live for a year and a half near Grasse, France.

1968   Film *Downhill Racer,* written by Salter.

1969   Films *The Appointment,* written by Salter, and *Three,* written and directed by Salter. Moves family to Aspen, Colorado.

1975   Divorced. *Light Years* published.

1976   Begins living with Kay Eldredge.

1979   *Solo Faces* published.

1980   Daughter Allan dies in accident. Moves back east to live on Long Island, occasionally spending summers in Colorado.

1982   Receives American Academy and Institute of Arts and Letters Award.

1983   Film *Threshold,* written by Salter.

1985   Son Theo born in Paris.

1986   House built in Bridgehampton, New York.

1987   Teaches in Iowa Writers' Workshop, fall semester.

1988   *Dusk and Other Stories* published. Begins pattern of living on Long Island in summer, Colorado in winter.

1989   Receives P.E.N./Faulkner Award. Teaches in Iowa Writers' Workshop, fall semester.

1991   Teaches at University of Houston, spring semester.

1997   *Burning the Days* published. Revised edition of *The Hunters* published. Teaches at Williams College, fall semester.

1998   Marries Kay Eldredge in Paris. Receives the John Steinbeck Award.

# Chapter One
# Early Years, Later Careers

When I asked James Salter in a letter in 1983 why his books were not written about more widely, he replied: "I suppose the reason I'm not much written about is that I've never had a book that sold well, and because Edmund Wilson, who I revere, is dead and probably wouldn't have liked me anyway. I hate letters like this, writers whining. They remind me of Farrell and Raymond Chandler and the writers in the Antaeus Poll of neglected books of the 20th century who listed their own. Every writer has a chance to his dying breath, and in a sense he should die with the pen falling from ink-stained fingers unless of course it's someone who has withdrawn from the lists. I like the inscription in Dr. Johnson's watchcase: *The night is coming when no man can work.*"[1] The literary vignettes are typical of Salter as is the mixture of confidence and self-effacement. Also characteristic is his refusal to complain about the vicissitudes of literary fame. Despite the lack of recognition of his work by the public, the academy, or a literary critic of Wilson's stature, Salter has not withdrawn from the lists. Now at 73 he is coming closer to "the night . . . when no man can work," but his fingers are still ink-stained. He is working on a novel, and he is taking notes and making preliminary sketches for a book about German artist Max Beckman, whose work he admires.

When I wrote to Salter in late 1996 requesting an interview, he suggested we meet in New York in early January, the time of a Beckman show at the Whitney Museum. A snowstorm delayed his trip from Colorado, however, and he arrived just after the exhibit had closed. We met at the Guggenheim instead. Salter was wearing a black turtleneck and a brown leather jacket as protection against New York's cold, and he graciously overlooked my being nearly 10 minutes late. He looked older than the picture in my mind, taken in 1989, but he still had the good looks, the short curly hair, and the step of an athlete, which took about a decade off his age. We walked up the museum's spiral and viewed the work of Ellsworth Kelly, huge canvases of monochromatic color in various shapes and angles. I did not have an artistic reference that could help me enjoy Kelly's work, and Salter consoled me by observing that it is only the validation the artistic community has given to Kelly's work that makes his art desirable. If these canvases were by the hands of an obscure laboring artist, no one would want to pay for or own them, and he nodded by way of example toward a square divided vertically into four equal panels of red, white, orange, and green. Salter rued our having missed the Beckman show, but he had been able to see it as it was being dismantled on the previous day thanks to a friend who knew the curator of the Whitney. Since I was unfamiliar with Beckman's work, we looked for and found an example on a postcard in the gift shop. Immediately I sensed Salter's enthusiasm and could appreciate the more accessible nature of Beckman's style, which reminded me of Rouault. Impressed as he was by seeing Beckman at the Whitney, Salter seemed even more moved by the handwritten notes attached to each painting, which detailed the work's condition, even the minutest irregularity, in a script both precise and sure. Curators use the notes to ensure safe handling, and their painstaking meticulousness signified for Salter a wonderful reverence for the artist's work, like the marginal commentary of some medieval monk on a sacred text.

The way that Salter described the curatorial notes reminded me of his own manuscript revisions to the typewritten copy of his books. When he scratches out a word, it is completely and evenly obliterated by a black bar, and his substitutions are penned with a sure artist's hand. Undoubtedly influenced by the drawing and painting he began in childhood—he still sketches occasionally—his handwriting is exact, concise, and flowing. So comely is his script that it expresses visually the author's veneration of words, their beauty and their potence. He composes his initial drafts in longhand and types them himself. To this day he is deaf to the siren promises of the computer, explaining that the conveniences of word processing do not appeal because the things it does so well, like instantly moving paragraphs or striking out and adding words, are tasks he likes doing manually. The time spent in correcting and recasting text by hand he considers time well spent, for such tasks, even the retyping of a manuscript, are exercises in reconsideration. Salter, in other words, enjoys the physical process of writing. "I'm a *frotteur,*" he says, "someone who likes to rub words in his hand, to turn them around and feel them, to wonder if that really is the best word possible. Does that word in this sentence have any electric potential? Does it do anything? Too much electricity will make your reader's hair frizzy. There's a question of pacing" ("Art," 59).

When Salter describes his method of writing, he compares its initial stages to an artist doing sketches of his subject. He will do quite a few preliminary ones before he begins a novel, often drawing on notes from his journals. Most of his material springs from experience, the source he believes of all great writing, but when that experience is not his own, as was the case with *Solo Faces,* which was inspired by the life of a young phenomenon in the world of mountaineering, he researches his subject and learns firsthand his métier, in this case mountain climbing.

Like most writers, Salter needs solitude, "preferably an empty house," in which to write, but unlike the majority, he feels no compulsion to go to his desk every day. Sometimes he is kept away by the press of affairs that require his attention, for he has had children around except during the years 1975 to 1985. Often though, he admits, "I just haven't brought myself to a position where I'm ready to write anything down" ("Art," 59). His very love of language precludes the daily grind of putting in the hours and hoping to salvage some gems from the junk. "I don't suppose," he says, "I can stand writing bad stuff. It's too painful."[2] On the other hand, when the mother lode is struck, he cannot be kept from the mine. When he was writing *A Sport and a Pastime* and *Light Years,* he was filled with an assurance, an urgency, and a nervous elation that drove the books to completion. Revision, of course, is crucial, and although some parts, like the opening of *A Sport and a Pastime,* are more resistant than others, he is patient in refining his work through revision after revision until the text glows with burnished devotion, reflecting the very sun. Finishing a book is a glorious thing. Salter tells of the night Styron completed *The Confessions of Nat Turner:* "It had happened at three in the morning in Connecticut. He went around and woke up all the children—they were small then—and sat them on the mantel-piece and put on Mozart. Never to be forgotten night" (*BD,* 203). Salter is the consummate writer both in the demands he makes of his own writing and in the homage, expressed mostly in such anecdotes, that he pays to other writers. He came to writing early in life, abandoned it when he donned a military uniform, and returned to it only after that commitment had run its 12-year course. What brought him full circle, more than anything else, was the belief, for him a true article of faith, that "life passes into pages if it passes into anything" (*BD,* 203).

James Salter came into the world as James Horowitz in Passaic, New Jersey, on 10 June 1925. His father was an engineer and real estate bro-ker, with degrees from West Point and MIT. He worked mainly in com-mercial real estate, always on the verge of striking the big deal, which never materialized. Salter's paternal grandfather lived at the Astor

Hotel when Salter was a boy. He was at one time part owner of a hotel near Saratoga Springs, New York, and had also been a toy importer, traveling often to Europe on business. Salter's mother's family—Scheff was her maiden surname—also had European roots, somewhere between Frankfurt and Moscow; exactly where has remained a matter of dispute among family members. On both sides of the family, it was Salter's grandparents who first came to America. Salter's mother grew up in Washington, D.C., where as a lively and beautiful young girl she graced country club dances and embassy balls. In her nineties, she continues to live in New York City.

The family moved to New York City when Salter was barely two years old, and he grew up there in a series of apartments, at first in a middle-class neighborhood on the West Side and later in the more posh upper East Side only a few blocks from the Metropolitan Museum and one block from Central Park. As a boy he painted and drew and read, mostly picture books at first; but later a six-volume collection called *My Bookhouse,* purchased from a door-to-door saleswoman in 1930, nourished the young boy's imagination with its folktales, poems, and softened versions of Dickens, Byron, the Bible, and Tolstoy. Kipling's "Ballad of East and West," with its code of fortitude and loyalty, was known by heart and became a scripture. Salter attended public grammar schools, even being allowed to walk to school alone as early as first or second grade. New York was such then that a schoolchild could do this. And pupils sat in rows in their classrooms according to merit, the best in front, where Salter generally found himself. By the middle grades, memorization and public recitation of poems were required, thus providing receptive students with an internal anthology of the language.

As an only child who was obedient to parents and in awe of his teachers, Salter spent his childhood placidly amid New York's bustle. The family was Jewish, but religion played only a minor role, so small that Salter's only reference to it in his memoir is a recollection of the practice at summer camp of saying the simple bedtime prayer "Now I lay me down to sleep." One summer the family went to the beach at Atlantic City to visit maternal relatives without Salter's father. The association of the carefree joy of that time with the smell and taste of the sea would later draw Salter back to live near the water's edge. If there was a shadow over his childhood, it was his father's self-absorption and apparent detachment. Salter remembers him as being generally preoccupied with grandiose plans, always prepared for the extravagant gesture and not afraid of taking risks. He rose steadily in his real estate transactions but suffered a number of financial calamities such as losing a $75,000 loan, given without collateral just before the crash of 1929 (*BD*, 203). Such losses eventually took their toll on his spirits and health.

Salter went to prep school from 1938 to 1942 at Horace Mann in Riverdale, a northern suburb, with a curriculum based on the classics, including required Latin, and a faculty composed almost entirely of men, mostly graduates of eastern colleges whose style was demanding and inflexible. One of these, an English teacher named Richard Wooster, who taught Salter in the 10th and 11th grades and was the adviser for the literary club, encouraged Salter's writing. Although Wooster did not exactly single Salter out and say, "You are the one," the two became close enough that they corresponded when Wooster served in the navy during the war. Much later, when he had published his first novel, Salter returned home to visit Wooster and show it to him. While in school Salter wrote for school publications, mostly poetry, won mention in a national poetry contest, and published poems in *Poetry* and *Scholastic* magazines. Although he was a good student, near the top of his class, Salter was not one dimensional. He played football a year or two behind another young man who would go on to literary fame, Jack Kerouac. Other schoolmates at Horace Mann were Julian Beck and John Simon. At graduation Simon received the Latin Scholar award while Salter was given the School Poet award. As the two left the stage, Salter said, "I didn't know you were a Latin scholar, John," and Simon replied, "I didn't know you were a poet."[3]

Among Salter's close friends from those days was a boy named Wink Jaffee. It proved an abiding friendship, and Wink's mother, Ethyl—an early image of the type of glamorous and self-sufficient woman that Salter has continued to admire—found an even deeper place in Salter's heart. Later Wink became a successful stockbroker and investor and was responsible in the 1950s for multiplying the money Salter received from the movie sale of his first novel, *The Hunters.*

The decision about where to go for college was complicated. Salter had been accepted at both Stanford and MIT, but his father, who had graduated first in his class from West Point, arranged a second alternate's appointment for his son. As a filial favor, Salter took the exam, never imagining the unlikely failure of both the principal and the first alternate. When the improbable happened, Salter recalls, "Seventeen, vain, and spoiled by poems, I prepared to enter a remote West Point" (*BD*, 44). In his autobiography, Salter describes his initial rebellion against the rigidity of a place that he compares in its dark passages and

Gothic facades to James Joyce's Clongowes Wood College. His defiance gradually diminished as Army ideals of leadership began to mesh with inner aspirations for manhood. The more he became an Army man, the more necessary it was to jettison his artistic side, for Cossacks did not write poetry. Eventually he embraced the military completely as a preparation for entering the ongoing struggle of World War II, which he remembers "claimed us and became, for me at least, the reality against which all future things would be judged."[4] Gone was the sad, uncertain and divided self, and in its place appeared "one that was unified and . . . right" (BD, 67).

These were formative years indeed. Salter began a lasting friendship with a born soldier among his classmates, and Kelton Farris would become "the face that remains" from those days (BD, 73). It was also the time of his first love affair, with a girl from a well-placed upper East Side family, someone he had known before. Salter's taste for fiction played a part in the romance as the young couple used a popular novel of the day, Shore Leave, as script for their love. When faced with an ultimatum from the young lady, however, about cementing their future together, Salter hesitated and lost her to another. Looking back he realized the significance of his inaction: "I had turned my back on three things, marriage, money, and the past, never really to face them wholeheartedly again" (BD, 86).

Before he graduated in 1945, the war in Europe ended. Ironically on 8 May, V-day, Salter got lost during a routine training flight for which the squadron was given incorrect winds aloft information. Unable to position himself and with a rapidly depleting gas supply, he attempted to land through midnight fog in a park in the middle of Great Barrington, Massachusetts. The plane crashed when one of its wings hit a treetop, wedging into the kitchen of a home where the family was in the midst of celebrating the return of a prisoner of war. Believing the low passes to be a military salute for their own hero, the family had all luckily rushed outside. The plane did not explode or catch fire because it was out of gas, so no one was hurt. Salter had his teeth and his pride shaken but otherwise was all right. After graduation came summer flight training in Texas, where the rumpled pilot was assigned to A-26s, attack bombers.

That August the war in the Pacific came to an end. Five months later Salter shipped there to fly transport planes, first in Manila, then Okinawa, and after three or four months, Honolulu. Unlike cadets from preceding classes, he was too late to be tested in the war he calls "the great forge of my time" (Letter, 1992).

Honolulu was basking in the romantic afterglow of the war. As Salter describes it then, it was a place of movie stars and "dancing under the palms, drinks on the lanai, boxing matches, idleness, summer clothes" (*BD*, 112). He was stationed at Hickam Field, still flying transports. There he became best friends with a captain who had been two classes ahead at West Point, and he fell in love with the captain's wife. The feelings were mutual, but the barriers of trust, honor, and conscience were insurmountable. "Nothing is as intense," Salter wrote of the affair, "as unconsummated love" (*BD*, 121). The trio were inseparable, and— although the intensity lessened when Salter and the couple were eventually stationed in different parts of the world—she left an indelible mark.

During Salter's West Point days, he had read widely if not deeply in literature, a distinguishing trait in a school whose universal major was engineering. His reading increased while he was in the Pacific. When hospitalized with blood poisoning from a cut incurred on a coral reef, he read all of Thomas Wolfe. Because any sign of intellectual activity, however, put one at risk of a desk job, he kept his literary interests to himself. He also began writing a novel in 1946, showing it to friends a year or two later when it was well advanced. One thought it rubbish, the other did not care for the title. He continued to work on it after returning to the States in 1948 to attend Georgetown University as a graduate student in international affairs. When he finished the novel, about a year later, he sent it to Harper Brothers, using a pen name, James Salter, because Air Force regulations at the time forbade publication of anything headquarters had not previously approved. Harper turned the manuscript down but liked it enough to ask to see his next.

In 1950 he received his master's degree from Georgetown, but the year marked an event that would begin an even more important education, Salter's first trip to Europe. Lured by his friend Kelton Farris's description of Paris in a letter as "all that anyone ever said it was, the showgirls don't believe in wearing clothes" (*BD*, 72), Salter visited him in Wiesbaden and drove with Farris and another officer to Paris. Nights of revelry followed days of discovery. Salter's schoolboy French allowed him to converse, and the city, still in the welcoming spirit of postwar bonhomie, smiled on American servicemen. Paris struck Salter like a revelation, and he felt himself heir to an unsuspected inheritance. The visit signaled, he said, the end of his formal education and the beginning of another kind, "not the lessons of school but something more elevated, a view of how to endure: how to have leisure, love, food, and conversation, how to look at nakedness, architecture, streets. . . . In Europe the shadow of history falls on you and, knowing none of it, you realize suddenly how small you are."[5] He discovered the censored books of the Olympia Press in a small tobacco shop, and he began to read widely in the European writers, eventually counting among his favorites André Gide, Louis-Ferdinand Céline, Henry de Montherlant, Jean Genet, and much later Isaac Babel. Europe henceforth would become a permanent recourse, Salter returning whenever possible throughout his life, often to rented houses in provincial towns.

In the summer of 1951, Salter married a young Washington, D.C. woman, Ann Altemus, whom he had met in Honolulu one afternoon in the courtyard of the Moana, a large hotel on Waikiki Beach, favored by tourists. Children followed, two girls born in 1955 (Allan) and 1957 (Nina). His Air Force career went to a different level in the year of his wedding. With the help of the general to whom he had been aide-de-camp, Robert M. Lee, at the atomic bomb tests at Eniwetok, Salter finally got his long-desired assignment to a fighter squadron, the 75th, in Presque Isle, Maine. As soon as he became adept in flying the F-86, then the Air Force's most advanced fighter, he volunteered for combat duty in Korea. When two openings came up early that winter, Salter and his best friend from the squadron, William Wood, went to Korea, where from February to July Salter flew more than a hundred combat missions. At the end of his tour of duty, he was credited with downing one MiG-15 and disabling another, hardly the five kills required to be an ace. In his autobiography he describes his disappointment: "Later I felt I had not done enough. . . . I had not done what I set out to do and might have done. I felt contempt for myself, not at first but as time passed, and I ceased talking about those days, as if I had never known them" (BD, 159). His Air Force career continued with assignments to fighter squadrons in the United States (1951–1953) and Germany (1954– 1957), where he became a squadron operations officer and briefly led an aerial acrobatic team at Bitburg.

Salter was an officer to his fingertips. Unlike John Cheever, who said, "That person in the army, that wasn't me," Salter reflects, "In my case, it was" (BD, 68); and he explains, "Like many prisoners, you come to love the prison and the other inmates. Cheever simply hadn't paid enough to have that feeling" ("Art," 75). Nevertheless, the publisher's reaction to Salter's first novel had been heartening, so he continued to write when he could, at night and on weekends. He finished a manuscript about the Korean War in 1955, and Harper Brothers took it, publishing The Hunters in 1956. Despite his attachment to the military life, it was the encouragement he needed to switch careers, harking back to a path he had abandoned when he entered West Point. Accordingly, vowing to write or perish, he resigned from the Air Force in 1957. With his wife and two children he moved to the Hudson Valley, first to Grandview, then in 1958 to New City in rural Rockland County.

In New York City, things were not going well. Salter's father was nearing the end of a steady decline of spirits that had begun more than 10 years before. He had been recalled to active duty during the war, serving at desk jobs in India and England. When the war ended and he returned to civilian life, he was never the same man. He felt things had changed too drastically on the business front: "The vice presidents of banks were no longer able to turn pieces of property over to you to work on, and there were no old widows who owned hotels and wanted the sale of them arranged" (*BD,* 33). He went to work for large corporations in New York and Chicago, but nothing clicked. The image of Willy Loman in *Death of a Salesman* comes to mind, a man out of step with the altered pace of the business world. Salter's father had always lived for the operatic moment, and cast into the wings, he was lost, beginning a gradual deterioration that led to financial ruin and despair. When he died in 1959, he was a broken man.

On the other side of town from the hospital where his father lay, Salter had found a room in which to write, a haven from the distractions of family and an antidote for suburban fever. He made the daily commute and wrote his second novel, *The Arm of Flesh.* While the book was being readied for publication, sometime in 1959, Salter, back in the country, tried to supplement his income by selling swimming pools. It was a distasteful and short-lived enterprise, but it did bring Salter into contact with a television writer by the name of Lane Slate. Neighbors in Rockland County, the two collaborated on a 12-minute documentary about collegiate football called "Team Team Team," which astonished its makers by winning a first prize at the Venice Film Festival in 1960. In 1961 appeared *The Arm of Flesh,* like its predecessor a novel about pilots and flying. Both books received decent reviews, with the most positive comments directed at Salter's style. Later, after both books had gone out of print, Salter, feeling they were not good enough, refused the offer of republication from North Point Press.

Even though he had switched careers, Salter continued to serve in the reserves, the Air National Guard. When the Berlin crisis came to a head in 1961, his unit was sent to France. While stationed at Chaumont in the Haute-Marne for 10 months in 1961 and 1962, he met Irwin Shaw through his agent, Max Wilkinson, who also happened to be Shaw's agent. Shaw was then in his late forties and had been living in Europe for a decade, playing host and patron to many young American writers like William Styron, Peter Matthiessen, and George Plimpton.

When Shaw wired Salter from Paris and suggested they meet for a drink in the bar of the Hotel Plaza Athénée one autumn night, the younger writer eagerly complied, driving "from the chill provinces by way of the thrilling diagonal that ran on the map from Chaumont, up through Troyes, to the very heart" (*BD*, 194). Despite Salter's tardiness due to a minor traffic scrape, Shaw was gracious, and the two hit it off, the literary lion in full possession of his fame and the novice brimming with a confidence beyond his accomplishments. Salter saw in Shaw a kind of father—his own had died only two years earlier—and a friendship started that lasted 28 years and involved Salter's naming a son "Shaw" and later flying across the Atlantic to be at the older writer's deathbed, only to miss by hours.

In 1962, back home from his tour of reserve duty, Salter became the father of twins, a girl named Claude and a boy named James Owen. Lane Slate and he continued their film work with a 10-part series about the circus for public television and with a documentary for CBS about contemporary American painters, an abiding interest of Salter since his youth. At this point the strands of Salter's writing overlap. With his 40th birthday approaching, he took stock of what he had written, found it wanting, and decided the time had come to show what he could do. Bolstered by the example of Ford Madox Ford, who at that age had felt similarly and written *The Good Soldier,* Salter sat down to work on notes he had made in 1961–62 during his stay in France. The result was his third novel, *A Sport and a Pastime,* which appeared in 1967. The book is Salter's ode to youth, desire, and provincial France—a poetic encroachment on sexual taboos. It marked Salter as a writer now no longer in aspiration but in fact. That same year the family went to the south of France to live in a large stone farmhouse, wonderful though unheated, in a village near Grasse.

Meanwhile, as a result of his success with documentaries and because his first novel had been made into a film starring Robert Mitchum, invitations from Hollywood began arriving in the mid-1960s. Lured by the financial prospects, excitement, and the challenge, Salter accepted. His debut as a film writer occurred when *Downhill Racer* (1968) with Robert Redford became a popular success. Two more films with scripts by Salter were released the following year: *The Appointment,* directed by Sidney

Lumet, and *Three,* based on a short story by Irwin Shaw, which Salter both wrote and directed. He had undertaken the project at Shaw's suggestion, but Shaw was never happy with the result even though the film was a success at the Cannes Film Festival.

Salter was writing at this time with the same brio with which a 21-year-old makes love. "At that period of life," he recalls, "I felt I could write anything: a sonnet, a libretto, a play" ("Art," 95). In 1968 his first published short story appeared in the *Paris Review,* and in the early 1970s three more would follow in its wake. One of the three, "The Cinema," is a cameo of a film shoot. Without marring the glamour that glosses the life of filmmaking, Salter reveals the underlying vanities and pretensions of its principals: actors whose every appearance demands an entrance and an exit, a director who must manipulate by subterfuge, flattery, and bravado. We can see in these stories Salter's preoccupation with personal issues. How good a writer was he? What constitutes selling out? How important is confirmation of one's art by another? In each of the stories appears the figure of a young writer who is struggling with his craft and trying to sort out its purity from surrounding distractions. Each of the artist figures relies on the love of a woman for confirmation of his art.

Salter's reputation as a lyric novelist took another step in 1975 with the publication of his fourth novel, *Light Years,* a story of conjugal bliss, family, and divorce. Its plot reflected what was happening at the time to Salter's own marriage, which came to an end the same year the novel was issued. Although *Light Years*'s critical reception was mostly favorable, Robert Towers's snide review in the *New York Times Book Review* (27 July 1975) likely hindered the book's sales, which were disappointing.

Salter began living in 1976 with Kay Eldredge, a writer of plays and journalism, and the two have been together since. They spend winters in Aspen, where Salter has been going since 1962, and summers in Bridgehampton on Long Island, where they built a house in 1986. As often as possible they have gone abroad, spending weeks, sometimes longer, in France, Italy, and England. One such visit to Paris in 1985 was timed to coincide with the birth of their son, Theo Shaw.

In 1977 Salter received an offer from Robert Redford to write a screenplay about mountain climbing. To understand the subject, Salter took it up in earnest, seeking out some of the sport's foremost practitioners and apprenticing himself. Although he had always been athletic, enjoying skiing, touch football, and tennis, nothing had prepared the 52-year-old neophyte for the challenging ordeal of serious rock and ice climbing. Salter based his film script on the story of a young American climber named Gary Hemming, who not long after some stunning climbs and a daring rescue in the Alps, killed himself. Redford did not like the result, and the film was never made. When a friend of Salter's, who happened to be editor in chief of Little, Brown, read the script, however, he offered the writer a contract to turn it into a novel. The result was *Solo Faces* (1979), capping Salter's novelistic output with another artistic success and popular disappointment, although the book sold better than his previous novels. The following year Salter's oldest daughter, Allan, died tragically in a freak electrical accident while in the shower. Salter was the one who found her. Thinking she had drowned, he attempted artificial respiration in vain. The memory remains so painful that this brief account of the accident in his memoir is all Salter has been able to write about it.

After more than 10 years of intermittent involvement in the movie business, Salter gradually extricated himself, like Melville's Bartleby, by escalating his "prefer nots": "I just said I would like to do less of this. I would like to do much less. I would like to do none of it" ("Art," 97). After *Solo Faces,* he routinely turned down movie offers, sending a printed card by return mail with his regrets. A couple of leftover commitments were all that remained of his film career. One of these eventuated into the movie *Threshold* (1983), and another was never made. The money earned from film scripts, however, dwarfed his previous income and left him feeling that movie writers "are among the most overpaid people on earth" ("Art," 97). Salter no longer hides his disdain for the movie business, and he looks back on his involvement like an old magician who now abjures the black magic he once practiced. He treats his films as if they were so many Calibans, hoping inquirers overlook such indiscretions.

Just as the novel had absorbed most of his writing attention in the 1970s, in the 1980s he focused on the short story. Six of his stories appeared in magazines, three each in *Esquire* and *Grand Street,* and by the end of the decade his collection, *Dusk and Other Stories* (1988), was published. *Dusk* earned the P.E.N./Faulkner Award, the most prestigious prize yet received by Salter. In 1986 he became a writer-in-residence for three weeks at Vassar. He taught thereafter at the Iowa Writers' Workshop in the fall of 1987 and 1989, and at the University of Houston during the spring of 1991. As enjoyable as was the contact with eager and ambitious youth, he found the preparation time immense, especially for a course he taught at Iowa on novels written by authors in their youth. His syllabus included *The Pickwick Papers, Sister Carrie, Typee, Dead Souls, Plain Tales from the Hills, Childhood/Boyhood/Youth* of Tolstoy, *Appointment in Samarra, A Portrait of the Artist as a Young Man,* and *Wise Blood.*[6]

Journalism has been another of Salter's occupations, beginning with assignments in the 1970s for *People* magazine, in which his interviews with Graham Greene, Vladimir Nabokov, and Antonia Fraser appeared. His journalistic essays on topics ranging from Eisenhower and European travel to open-heart surgery and relationships between older men and younger women have appeared in the *New York Times, Esquire, Gentleman's Quarterly, Vogue, Geo, Traveler,* and *Life.* Although he has long relied on journalism as a source of income, still writing occasional pieces like "The Dos and Don'ts of Aspen" (*Esquire,* January 1996), his journalistic output has lessened over the years.

In 1986, impelled by an autobiographical article he wrote for *Esquire,* Salter began a memoir that has been his major artistic focus in the 1990s. His original contract with Random House called for a 1989 publication date, but the labor has been lovingly slow and the completion oft delayed. A number of the chapters have appeared as essays, like the piece on his West Point days, "You Must" (*Esquire,* December 1992), which was anthologized in *Best American Essays 1993.* Salter completed the manuscript of *Burning the Days* in late 1996, and in September 1997 Random House brought out a first edition of 35,000 copies, Salter's largest to date. I spoke with him just after the manuscript had been sent to the publisher, and he remarked on just how much of his life is not covered in the book and how he could write another remembrance without even touching the events in this one. Such, however, is not his intention. He has revised his first novel, *The Hunters,* which Counterpoint has issued in a new hardcover edition (1997). In the mid-1990s a number of Salter's novels have been released abroad, notably *A Sport and a Pastime,* which has at last been translated into French, as well as *Light Years.* The European reviews have been glowing. In the fall of 1997, Salter returned to the academy, occupying an endowed chair at Williams College in western Massachusetts.

In 1998, Salter and Eldredge married in Paris. They continue to divide their time between Bridgehampton and Aspen, where their 13-year-old son goes to school. In each location Salter has his writing study, a cabin apart from the main house in Aspen and an airy second-floor office with a peaked ceiling in Bridgehampton. In each place there are paths on which Salter can walk Paavo, his Welsh corgi, a breed he favors for its independence and individuality. He relishes the life he is living but still hopes to see a book of his become popular, having grown a bit tired of the mantle of a "writer's writer." When I asked him at the end of our last interview what advice he would give to young writers, Salter answered: "I'd say it's worth it. Try to believe. Young writers want love, admiration, and glory, but they must consider that they may carry within the thing that is important."[7] It was almost as if he were talking to himself, shoring up his own faith in the value of his writing and its ultimate recognition by others.

# Chapter Two
# Pilot and Novelist
## (The Hunters, The Arm of Flesh)

Even though James Salter did not fight in World War II, it profoundly influenced his life. Not quite 17, he had graduated from Horace Mann just six months after the bombing of Pearl Harbor. He entered the United States Military Academy the following fall guided by filial duty and perhaps fate. He had leaned toward attending Stanford, never imagining that as a second alternate he would be admitted to West Point. When he was, he could not say no, for his father's record there had been the one distinguishing mark of his life. Dreamy, romantic, or, as Salter put it, "spoiled by poems," he obligingly headed for the academy on the Hudson with mixed feelings. He was unprepared for the regimentation, the traditions, and the discipline of the military school. At first he resisted, chafing under the rigors, but as the war intensified and men left the Point to become heroes in it, his ideals began to take a shape almost identical to the Army's own. Salter's imagination, and that of his generation, had been fired by the books about the first war, *All Quiet on the Western Front* and *A Farewell to Arms,* which provided stirring portraits of heroism. Now the curtain had opened on a new war, and the roles were being cast. The stage metaphor, in fact, informed public consciousness as indicated by the common references to the European and Pacific war zones as "theaters." The audience was the entire country, which applauded when one of their own came into the spotlight, and applauded even louder if the appearance was tragic. To be immortalized, in life or in death, in such an arena, only courage was needed.

Coincidentally, Salter's first brush with death occurred on the very day the war in Europe ended, 8 May 1945. It was not in combat, however, and it was anything but glorious. Because the winds had been incorrectly forecast for this routine training mission out of Stewart Field, near Newburgh about 40 minutes from West Point, the entire squadron got lost. Unlike the others, however, Salter was unable to get his bearings. He tried all the advice in the booklet "What to Do If

Lost," but he could not right himself. When his dwindling gas supply finally forced him to attempt a landing, he had no idea where he was or that the park he had picked out through the Great Barrington, Massachusetts, fog was dotted with trees. By all rights he should have been killed when the plane's wing clipped one of these and he crashed into a nearby house. His empty gas tank, however, had saved him, just as the misinterpretation of his low passes overhead had saved the house's occupants. Without a fire or an explosion, Salter walked away from the crash, his bones shaken and a tooth broken but otherwise intact.

The war in the Pacific ended in August 1945 while Salter, now graduated, was in Austin, Texas. He writes of the event: "In one bold stroke we were devalued, like currency, and for nearly six months were transferred from field to field, to bases ever more bleak and—the aircraft mechanics having been demobilized—silent" (BD, 104). He would go to the Pacific theater, but not until six months after the show had closed. Can youth today appreciate the yearning for battle that surged through the young men of war age in the 1940s as it had in the 1910s? Salter, in a tribute to Dwight D. Eisenhower, wrote how when the first war had ended with Eisenhower still in training assignments, "he had suffered the classic grief of young officers—he had not seen action."[1] The poignancy of this grief is distilled in *Burning the Days* when Salter describes sailing out of San Francisco, passing under the Golden Gate Bridge, and turning back to read the huge banner strung across it to greet the returning troops: "Welcome Home, Heroes" (BD, 105).

Having missed the war he esteemed "the reality against which all future things would be judged" ("Infamy," 23L), Salter began his 12-year Air Force career in Manila, a city that was half destroyed. The residue of war was ugly: palm trees whose tops had been blown off, broken and rusted equipment, slack discipline, and the prevalence of theft and other vices. The fighter planes were badly maintained and needed to be flown correctly to avoid mishaps, resulting in frequent accidents that were usually deadly. But Salter was assigned to transports, which had few crashes. In July of 1946, he was transferred to Hickam Field in Honolulu, remaining in transports but flying further distances.

Two intense love affairs occurred at this time. The first involved Salter's pursuit of a girl he had met at one of the last dances held at West Point. She was dancing with someone else when Salter saw her for the first time and he was overwhelmed. He boldly cut in on the dance and made enough of an impression to get her phone number. Dates followed, but before long Salter was sailing to the Philippines. During the voyage he discovered, to his dismay, that his competitors were many, at least three of them on the same ship. Nevertheless, by means of letters, intermediaries, and several visits back to New York, where the girl worked for a fashion illustrator, in the course of two years "her love was slowly given and deeply held" (*BD*, 107). The grip of this love, however, was loosened when Salter met another woman on the base in Honolulu who stunned him. Unfortunately she was the wife of a fellow officer and close friend. In the way of such things, the captain's wife eclipsed his former flame. Although "Paula," the name Salter uses for his new love in his memoir, felt the same about Salter, they recognized that their love's normal course was blocked by rules of friendship and loyalty, leaving a vacuum in Salter's life. Paula chose to fill this vacuum rather unconventionally but definitively by selecting for him a suitable mate, someone Salter had met among the vacationing tourists in the courtyard of one of the great hotels. True to the script, Salter pursued the choice and eventually married her in 1951.

One day in the surf at Kwajelein, Salter cut his foot on a coral reef and had a nasty battle with the resulting poison. During his slow convalescence, he discovered Thomas Wolfe and his powerful waves of words. About the same time he began to write a novel himself, which he finished in 1948 after he had returned to the States for graduate studies in international affairs at Georgetown. The novel was rejected, but in an encouraging manner by Harper Brothers, who invited him to send along his next endeavor.

In 1951 Salter's Air Force career was raised to an altogether different level when he was finally assigned to the 75th Fighter Squadron. He took to the F-86 as if he had been born to fly it, and when the opportunity presented itself, he volunteered for combat in Korea, joining the 335th Fighter Squadron from February to July of 1952, where he flew more than a hundred missions. In combat Salter starkly confronted his ideals of heroism, downing one MiG and escaping a number of close calls. Although his combat performance was never enough in his own judgment (for years he stopped talking altogether of Korea), he possessed the role of fighter pilot so completely that he could later write about it without irony. After Korea came assignments in the United States and Germany. On weekends, days off, and at night, he resumed writing. In 1953 he began to jot down notes for a novel about flying in Korea and wrote most of *The Hunters* from 1954 to 1955. He dedicated

the book to "W who was my friend," William Wood, with whom he had
shared both cadet life and combat in Korea.

## The Hunters

Whatever the merits or defects of his first novel, it carries the unmistakable stamp of authenticity. Salter's firsthand combat flying against Russian MiGs over North Korea qualifies as one of those powerful and
unusual life events that propel potential writers into print. As he says in
the novel's early pages, "It was still all adventure, as exciting as love, as
frightening."[2] Great literature may not result from such occasions, but
the writers, often young, may be forgiven, for their stories must chase
the powerful train of experience. Melville's career began with such an
adventure and such a book. His exploits, jumping ship in the Marquesas
Islands and living among a tribe of cannibals, were so innately dramatic,
even startling, they required telling. Audiences liked the exoticism of
*Typee* so much that they clamored for Melville to repeat the adventure in
every book.

Salter's Korean experience in the Air Force's F-86, the only jet then
capable of challenging the Russian MiG-15 in the sky, informs and ani-
mates *The Hunters*. The book's protagonist, Cleve Saville in the original
edition (note the closeness of the last name to the author's), an experienced pilot who has not yet been tested in combat but of whom much is
expected, is James Salter in all the important ways. In the revised edition, Salter changed Cleve's surname to Connell, why I do not know
unless he wished to obscure the connection.[3] Like Salter, Cleve is a natural when it comes to flying. Also like Salter, he is older than most of
the pilots in Korea at 31 (Salter had been 27), having already learned "a
little of silence and perhaps devotion" (*H,* 8). Cleve comes to the air war
in Korea as if it were an authentication of manhood, wanting to prove
himself the war hero his father expects him to be. Salter, in his autobiography, writes about himself and his friend Wood racing to volunteer for
Korea: "[T]he war itself was whispering an invitation: Meet me. Whatever we were, we were inauthentic. You were not anything unless you
had fought" (*BD,* 132).

The single criterion for validation in *The Hunters* is downing enemy
aircraft. Although damaged MiGs are a credit, the confirmed kill alone
merits a star next to the pilot's name on the squadron list. A pilot's reputation grows with his number of stars, and "if you shoot down five
planes you join a group, a core of heroes. Nothing else can do it" (*H,*

135). Although Cleve Connell enters the fray with confidence and is quickly made a flight commander because of his recognized skill, the victories simply do not materialize. His missions encounter few MiGs, and when they do, the MiGs are either too far away or too unaggressive to engage. Connell's assurance becomes strained when uneventful flights multiply while a cocky neophyte flies irresponsibly but with stunning results, quickly downing his first enemy jet and subsequently adding others to his total. Ed Pell's arrogance and opportunism are poised against Connell's quiet confidence and bad luck, but Connell knows blaming luck is only a fool's consolation. Pressure mounts on Cleve, for "everybody was waiting for proof of his ability, and somehow he had not been able to give it" (*H,* 71). Yet he refuses to reduce his ambition, knowing that, unlike the others, "[h]e had not come merely to survive" (*H,* 35).

Connell's refusal to abandon that one taut value that served as the "single definition of excellence" (*H,* 72) is rewarded when he does down his first MiG. "Cleve had never felt so fine as when finally they headed back through the quiet sky. This was the real joy of it all. He understood at last" (*H,* 85). With the terrible weight of inconsequence removed, Cleve is able to relax, taking a recreational leave in Tokyo with DeLeo, another pilot.[4]

The Tokyo interlude of four chapters divides the book in half and offers a welcome change of pace and mood from the intensity of war. It also introduces the themes of pleasure, art, and love that run throughout Salter's work, widening the book's somewhat narrow focus on achieving glory through military prowess. At Tokoshi's, an elite Tokyo brothel, the two men are pampered, bathed, and served. Here, as elsewhere in his works, Salter limns these pleasures of the flesh briefly and effectively: "She caressed him beneath the water. She presented herself to him deliberately. They laughed at nothing. They played like children in the steamy room. In the thick bedroll on the tatami floor, she was as obliging as a new wife. He woke up twice during the night. She was instantly awake and seemingly pleased both times" (*H,* 115). It is no wonder that in her *The Joy of Writing Sex* Elizabeth Benedict singles out Salter for praise, recognizing that he "writes with extraordinary elegance and compression about sex."[5] The stark but revealing details in Salter's sexual encounters carry enormous conviction. In this incident, after the men awake in the morning to another hot bath, Salter conveys the satisfaction, the leisure of it all as they linger under the spell of pleasure and "see the tips of distant smokestacks with their blackened mouths beginning to issue smoke as the working day started for lesser men" (H, 115). Satiety such as this often is hedged in Salter's writing with a realization of the limits of the experience. Here it is limited by its uniqueness and therefore unrepeatability, and that is why Cleve tells DeLeo, "[W]e should never come back here," for to do so would be only a vain attempt to recapture the past. Such satisfaction also is limited by its brevity and therefore serves as a reminder of life's brevity. Cleve is impelled to think of death in the midst of pleasure, opining, "The way to go is in an instant, reaching for that highest one of the stars and then falling away, disappearing, against the earth. I wouldn't mind that, would you?" (H, 116). The reflection clearly puts this interlude of pleasure in the context of a larger striving, and when DeLeo reminds Cleve, "In this greatest life of yours, you have to win" (H, 116), it suggests that pleasure alone is insufficient for some, that the fruit of pleasure would rot without attachment to the tree of accomplishment.

The second movement of the Tokyo interlude brings Cleve to the home of an artist, Mr. Miyato, introducing another of the prominent themes of Salter's writings, the elevating quality of art. Whenever writers feature a visual artist in a novel or short story, one should take particular notice of how the artist's work is described, for most likely it will mirror the intentions of the writer's own work. Such is the case here as Salter describes the strong impression of Miyata's canvases on Cleve: "The work of years was here in a style muted but commanding. He had never seen anything like them. The colors were dominated by blue and gray with Oriental mood and pose. Many were nudes, some life size. The eye slid from their frankness, but still they were so religious, with such patient, calm devotion, that Cleve felt himself held undisturbedly before them" (H, 128). The details correspond to important elements of Salter's work as it would develop over the years: the style both muted and commanding, the frankness of subject matter, especially the nudes, if you will, of A Sport and a Pastime, and above all the reverential devotion, both calm and patient, that Salter would lavish on the beautiful things of earth, his sacramentalizing of the profane. After being exposed to such visual delights and to Miyata's intelligent conversation, Cleve is elevated, realizing the life of creation is as marvelous as the life of physical pleasure. Salter writes, "Cleve felt he had somehow entered a level of the city that he had not imagined existed" (H, 128). And when Miyata tells Cleve the story behind his career, how nearly all his works were destroyed in the bombing of Tokyo and how he began again from scratch, Cleve sees that courage is a universal, as valuable in art as in combat.

The final revelation of the interlude is the importance of love. Miyata's daughter, Eico, walks into the room and "as he saw her clearly for the first time, Cleve knew that the moment would be one of the few remaining to the end" (*H,* 130). Younger than he at 19 and splendid in her black hair and carriage, Eico's beauty wounds Cleve immediately, but it is the afternoon's mutual unfolding of their secrets that separates this experience from the earlier one with the obliging prostitute. Time allows the couple only the Eden of a spring afternoon on the shores of a lake, not enough occasion even for consummation, but enough for "wild hopes of being able to give completely and receive in equal measure—visions, dizzying dreams, quills of desire"[6] and enough for Cleve to register this among his permanent treasures: "In the spring afternoon they lay, the light falling on them. There was no future or past. There was the slow, immortal beating of his blood, somehow in time with hers he wanted to imagine" (*H,* 135).

Cleve ends the holiday abruptly when he hears that a major air battle has ensued with casualties on both sides. The interlude is over, and the focus again returns to the scramble for glory that grips Cleve, his need to win. His ambition is intensified by the return to the war of the legendary Russian ace, nicknamed Casey Jones, with the distinctive black stripes on his MiG. And Connell's pride is piqued by the continuing rise of the arrogant Pell, who now has three kills. Pell, however, continues to cause problems for the rest of the group by his unpredictability. On Cleve's first mission back, he is forced to break off from a certain kill in order to cover Pell, who was calling for help, only to observe Pell record his fourth victory. Now certain that Pell is destined to become an ace, Cleve is forced to reevaluate his own ambitions, which seem cheapened by Pell's proximity to achieving them. There ensues an inner struggle about the whole numerology of heroism: "He had come for a climax of victory, but in a way he did not want that now. He wanted more, to be above wanting it, to be independent of having to have it" (*H,* 161). Yet, despite this wish for detachment, Cleve knows he is incapable of it, that he is "a prisoner of war," and that if he does not shoot down MiGs he will fail in his own and others' eyes (*H,* 161).

Pell becomes an ace on his next mission, in a more disturbing way than in any of his other triumphs because it is at the expense of losing another pilot whom he should have been covering and warning of danger. This victory—tarnished only in the eyes of Cleve and DeLeo, who know the facts—raises Pell into the hallowed circle of heroes. His name joins the other legends of battle. For Cleve the coronation is undigestible, for this hated unworthy has fulfilled the very goal to which Cleve has aspired in vain. Now, however, with his tour of duty winding down and his ambition trumped by Pell, Cleve conceives an even more ambitious prize, something no one has even come close to accomplishing, downing Casey Jones. He thinks, "One clean mark for them all to see. To kill a champion. To know once more the breadth of excellence, compared to which everything else was dross" (H, 178).

When given the chance, Cleve proves worthy, diving through low clouds toward the earth in chase of the black-striped MiG, risking all, and finally lacing the Russian plane with shots and watching it plunge to the ground. Connell finds his glory, the thing he had dreamed of, but he does not claim it. Instead, in an even greater act of selflessness, he credits the kill to his wingman, Billy Hunter, whose plane had crashed short of the field, because "Hunter had once told him that he would rather have his [name] there [on the operations chart] than anything else in the world" (H, 91). In relinquishing his personal glory, Connell proves superior to his own ambition, fulfilling the one thing lacking in his manhood and leadership, detachment. By glorifying his dead comrade, Connell finds "his destiny and godliness" in a vision more authentic than his original ideal.

Almost as a coda to the novel, which really climaxes in Cleve's triumph of courage and character, Salter ends with two scenes skillfully tied together. A reporter is interviewing Pell for a national magazine, which will almost certainly promulgate Pell's fame, when word comes that Connell's plane has been seen going down. The reporter asks about Connell, and Pell answers with false generosity and false modesty that Connell was Pell's mentor and that he "taught me everything I know about this business" (H, 232). The book then closes with a thirdhand report of Cleve's own end, shot down by enemy fighters "with that contagious passion peculiar to hunters" (H, 233). Cleve goes to his death, alone knowing the secret of his triumph, while Pell is destined to be celebrated for his flying prowess as well as for his magnanimity. Glory, Salter implies, is not always what it seems.

Reviewers recognized the authenticity of the novel's adventures and praised the author's aplomb in making the whole experience of combat flying accessible to readers. George Barrett, writing in the *New York Times,* thought the novel had "none of the hokum that (for the sake of specific comparison with recent popular Korean war tales) marks James Michener's output."[7] Taliaferro Boatwright in the *New York Herald Tribune* called it "an astonishingly fine novel";[8] and S. P. Mansten in *Saturday Review* said, "Some of the flight scenes are models of tense description and the whole story is filled with authentic details in the lives of men who face death on wings."[9]

The novel is well constructed and brisk, the writing mostly firm and effective, especially in the revised edition. There are still a few lapses, but they are the kind generated by youth, such as when Salter overly dramatizes Cleve's early soul-searching: "He had never been beaten, and it would not happen now. . . . The mystic tissue that joined the soul of a man together, he felt it dissolving" (*H,* 73). Given the previous comparison of Cleve's despair to a football defeat on the road, it all sounds mawkish and a bit adolescent. Overall, though, *The Hunters* is a cleaner book in its newly revised edition. Salter has pruned away some of the excesses of his youthful zest, but he has not tried to suppress the enthusiasm altogether, for part of the book's charm, after all, is its youthful voice. He did not tinker with the ending, although it is rather inconsistent to abandon Cleve's perspective for a thirdhand account of his death. Up until then, his was the central consciousness of the novel, and the reader was privy to his thoughts. Suddenly Cleve's interiority at this crucial and dreaded moment is denied the reader, a disconcerting and artificial change in point of view, which is done, it seems, for the sake of an ironic, as opposed to a melodramatic, ending. The irony, indeed, is effective as we are left with the contrasting images of Pell and Connell, images of hollow and real heroism.

In the past, Salter, a stern judge of his own performance, has been prone to dismiss both of his early novels as works of youth, little worth serious consideration. His recent decision to revise *The Hunters,* however, suggests a revision of that appraisal as well, at least as regards his first novel. This will please readers like Samuel Hynes, who in a recent review of Salter's memoir in the *New York Times Book Review,* urged the author to reverse his "harsh judgment" on his early novels, for "who has written better fiction about men in planes?" (Hynes, 9). Indeed, as first novels go, *The Hunters* is nothing to be ashamed of. It captures the air war and the mind of the would-be hero with vivid accuracy and suspense. The writing is authoritative, and the story is nicely paced and well structured, introducing seamlessly themes that will recur throughout Salter's corpus. The lonely quest for glory that transpires in the rarefied air over Korea will find other contexts in later stories and novels. In fact, each of Salter's novels plays a different variation on the theme of man's desire for glory in the face of death.

The publication of his first novel, spiced by a favorable critical reception, was all the omen Salter needed to switch careers. He resigned his Air Force commission with the rank of major in 1957, on his 32nd birthday, having been in uniform since he was 17. Salter had been a pilot to his fingertips, giving himself completely to the life, so the break was wrenching. He had stayed in the Air Force as long as he did because there was a beauty, a purity in the life; and as a regular officer and West Point graduate with combat experience, he was part of an elite corps. On the day he was to resign, he roamed the Pentagon, nearly ill, with the grim resolve of someone filing for a divorce before finally submitting his letter. He recalls, "Everything I had done in life up to that point, I was throwing away. I felt absolutely miserable—miserable and a failure" ("Art," 74). The misery ultimately stemmed from the scale of Salter's military ambition. Like Cleve Connell, he had aspired to greatness in war. Having been denied that, he stayed in the Air Force because he believed in its ideals, and he hoped that somehow, if he remained ready, he might be called to a larger role. It would happen eventually to Salter's fellow pilots Ed White, Buzz Aldrin, and Virgil Grissom. In 1956, however, the publication of Salter's first novel opened a whole new possibility for lasting achievement. Salter had rejected his artistic, poetic self when he embraced the military life at West Point. Now, because literary accomplishment seemed a genuine possibility, he reversed himself and jettisoned the military man he had become.

With a wife and two small children, and with the determination "to write or perish," Salter settled near the Hudson River in the suburbs north of New York City. In 1958, seeking solitude to write, he found a room in the lower right-hand corner of Manhattan on Peck Slip, a neighborhood near the fish market that was cheap enough to house a number of poor but hopeful artists. To this room, with its bare wooden floor and scarred windowsills, he commuted daily and worked on his second novel. Salter has always drawn heavily on personal experience in his writing, and this tale continued to plunder his Air Force days. What else did he have? Also the emotional attachment had been strong, hardly exhausted by one book. As he later would write in his memoir about the Air Force: "I ate and drank it, went in whatever weather on whatever day, talked its endless talk, climbed onto the wing to fuel the ship myself, fell into the wet sand of its beaches with sweaty others and was bitten by its flies, ignored wavering instruments, slept in dreary places, rendered it my heart" (*BD*, 185).

## *The Arm of Flesh*

*The Arm of Flesh* seeks then to capture the life of pilots in a fighter squadron stationed in Germany, where Salter had served for four years. Unlike its predecessor, however, which dealt with wartime flying, this novel is about "the peacetime routine. Africa for gunnery once a year, the deserted coast. Munich from time to time to stand alert. The rest in the Rhineland, straightening things out, falling into habit, then packing again to go."[10] The subject matter is more amorphous than *The Hunters*, which was given focus and drama by its protagonist's search for glory in the cauldron of war. Here there is no protagonist, no wartime drama, and no central search. Nor is there a single narrative voice. Instead, Salter uses 17 different narrators, 9 of whom speak only once. Three characters deliver half of the monologues: Captain Isbell has 16 appearances on center stage; the squadron commander, Major Clyde, is next with 7; and Lieutenant Sisse has 5. Inspired by Faulkner's successful use of multiple narrators in *As I Lay Dying*, a book he admired, Salter gambled on this unusual narrative technique as a way to explore facets of the peacetime experience of Air Force pilots in Europe after the war. Faulkner had shown how apt the technique was to convey the subjectivity of experience. Similarly Salter uses the multiple narrators to function like photographs of flying and base life from different angles, in varying light, from different perspectives. Faulkner's great novel, however, had two important focusing elements Salter's book lacks: its central journey to bury Addie Bundren and the close-knit family circle around which the drama unfolds. By contrast, the action of *The Arm of Flesh* is divided among a number of different landings and takeoffs by members of a U.S. fighter squadron in Europe, the fabric of daily life on the bases, and the changes in weather—none of which provides a center.

The novel begins with planes attempting to land in low cloud cover, and the final dramatic incident is similar with two pilots, arguably the book's most pivotal characters, attempting a near blind landing, one without radio contact. Captain Isbell and Lieutenant Cassada hardly provide the weblike interrelatedness that the Bundren family gives to *As I Lay Dying*, but they do offer some focus. Isbell, the operations officer and the most frequently recurring narrator, imparts to the book a continuity and dominant tone, which he sounds most noticeably when, nearing the end of his tour of duty, he reminisces: "This time of year in Munich, the Isar is running under the bridges. I see it pouring along, pale green, bringing the city to life. What do they feel flying down and seeing maybe the last snow of winter lying in seams along the ground? Then coming in high over the blue city with its streets invisibly thronged? The sweet anticipation. The joy. My thoughts are swirling. I see everything, faces for the last time, dancers at the *Palast,* streets at midnight, Sunday afternoons" (*AF,* 182). The book is guided by Isbell's nostalgic spirit, which is one with Salter's, who gave himself over completely to flying and Air Force life. Isbell's name, like Saville's in the first edition of *The Hunters,* repeats the double syllabic pattern and the "S" and "L" consonants of the author's surname. Also, like the author's alter ego in his first novel, Isbell is 31 years old and takes seriously his mission of leadership, seeing himself as a kind of peacetime Moses guiding his men "within sight of what was promised" (*AF,* 15). Salter too, as is clear from his memoir, had aspired to the ideals of such leadership in his military days.

Cassada is the most difficult of all the flock to lead and is written off by the squadron commander, although Isbell refuses to give up on him. Unlike the other pilots featured in the novel, Cassada has no monologues, some distinction in itself, indicating that his importance lies less in his impression of events than in his impact on others and in his fate, which is tragic. Cassada is the overconfident upstart who cannot master the task but whose aspiration and competitiveness portend danger. Captain Wickenden, having seen the type, senses "the mark of death" on Cassada and predicts disaster. Since Wickenden, however, is thoroughly cynical, one does not know whether to trust his prophecy. Isbell dismisses Wickenden's fatalism, finding potential in Cassada and wanting to "bequeath him my dreams" (*AF,* 98). Cassada is a litmus test for the others, who reveal something of themselves in their reaction to him. For Major Clyde, Cassada is immediately devalued by his demeanor, which was not "roaring" or "full of hell" enough to resemble Clyde's memory of himself at the same age. And Cassada's fate is sealed for the major when he insists on having tea instead of coffee, a sign of unmanliness. In his portrait of Clyde, Salter shows us the careerist who is interested more in his own swaggering image than in true leadership. Lieutenant Harlan is another who takes a dim view of Cassada, egging him into a desperate bet on gunnery scores. For Harlan, Cassada is all posturing and little performance, and he punishes Cassada's pride by pushing the bet up to a month's salary. Although Cassada fails to win the bet, he does show significant improvement in his gunnery scores, earning some respect. Sensing his promise, Isbell selects him for an assignment in North Africa, hoping that Cassada's eagerness will eventuate in performance. It never does. When Isbell and Cassada return from Africa, Isbell's radio goes out and he is forced to signal Cassada to lead, following closely on his wing. The weather worsens, and clouds thicken ominously as the pair approach their home base with fuel dwindling rapidly. All depends on Cassada and his ability to bring in his and Isbell's aircraft on instructions from the tower. After three missed passes and aborted landings, Isbell loses sight of Cassada's plane and is left no choice in his blind flight through low cloud cover but to eject. On Cassada's final approach his fuel and luck run out, and he plunges to his death. Salter builds the same taut suspense into this landing that he created in the battles in *The Hunters*. The only revelation here, however, is that some people like Cassada do seem doomed. Wickenden was right. Despite the disaster, however, Isbell was also right in trying to impart something of value to Cassada, something that would give him the chance to succeed.

The novel continues Salter's preoccupation with the responsibilities of leadership, and Isbell, like Cleve Connell, proves himself a true leader despite the results. Salter had studied leadership at West Point and had formed an ideal to which he had aspired in his own military service. A leader was "someone whom difficulties could not dishearten, privation could not crush. It was not his strength that was unbreakable but something deeper, his spirit . . . someone whose life was joined with that of his men, who had reached the peak of the human condition, *admired, feared, and loved,* someone hardened and uncomplaining, upon whom the entire struggle somehow depended, someone almost fated to fall" (*BD,* 65–66).

This ideal may have been the most difficult thing that Salter left behind when he resigned from the Air Force. One of the pilots he had flown with in Germany, Ed White, would later become the first American to walk in space, dwarfing by his achievement all of Salter's desire for fame. The author writes in his memoirs about watching White's space walk from a Paris hotel, "sick with envy—he was destroying hope. Whatever I might do, it would not be as overwhelming as this" (*BD,* 165). It was the loss of such possibilities and the loss of the patrician experiences of being a fighter pilot that Salter was feeling when he wrote his two early novels. In *The Hunters,* he focused on the combat side of this experience, showing "a way to live and a way to die" (*H,*

106). In *The Arm of Flesh,* he was trying to immortalize the generic nature of the pilots' experience while showing its individual nuances. He reveals the subtle yet absolute differences between the true leader, here Isbell, and the cardboard leader, Major Clyde, who is more interested in the way his superiors perceive his command than in the men themselves and their mission.

The problem with the book is that there are too many speakers and too little plot. The constant shifts in perspective, although one understands their motivation, so interrupt narrative flow that the reader must continually reconstruct context. As a result, no story line is established, only a situation and the experiences of individuals in this situation, namely an American fighter squadron stationed in Germany. One is given glimpses, piecemeal, of the competitive ways of fighter pilots, the boredom of wives, the transcendence that accompanies flying, and the uneasy solace of relationships between pilots and local girls. What is lacking, however, is a central thread that would go beyond takeoffs and landings, no matter how dangerous and dramatic these are made by conditions of weather or faulty instrumentation. Salter tries to compensate for this lack of continuity by having many of his speakers circle about shared concerns, principally Cassada. Lieutenant Sisse is another who comments frequently about "the problem boy" (*AF,* 63). Sisse, more sympathetic than the others, broadens the picture of Cassada, for he observes Cassada's other life—his frequent visitations to a girlfriend in Munich—which imparts to the doomed airman a luster unrecognized by most of his fellow pilots. So moved is Sisse by this side of Cassada that he admits, "We are drawn toward the paths of planets mysterious and never regain our own" (*AF,* 104). The mystery of Cassada, however, is never explored, and too many questions are left unanswered. Sisse's private emotions are among the many loose ends never tied together into what Chaucer called the "knotte" of a story. Sisse, in fact, disappears from the narration after the preceding tribute midway through the novel.

Other threads are also left undeveloped, like the marital lives of Major Clyde, whose wife, Ernestine, is having an affair with Lieutenant Godchaux and likely others, and Captain Isbell, whose wife, Marion, recoils from sex. Both women have monologues, adding the wives' perspective to this multidimensional picture of base life. After a tryst with Godchaux on the forest floor, Ernestine thinks of herself as "Ernestine, the lieutenants' delight. Makes men of them. Just like her husband" (*AF,* 165–166). In Isbell's marriage, it is he who strays, admitting in his last monologue that he has been seeing a girl, Marriane, who works at the officer's club in Munich. Such revelations, however, do not coalesce. They lead nowhere, remaining interesting but isolated facts in the lives of pilots and wives.

Although reviewers did not seem to know what to make of the novel, they treated it kindly. *Kirkus* was satisfied with the description of the book as an "experimental novel" whose technique was "deliberately oblique."[11] Taliaferro Boatwright in the *New York Herald Tribune* called it "an intricate and masterful suspense story."[12] Only he among the reviewers ventured to sort out the book's "discontinuous series of monologues" as a story of one man's "fumbling attempt to break out of the mold, to communicate" (Boatwright, 1961, 29). Even Boatwright, though, felt that the book's most significant part—the relationship between Isbell and Cassada—"comes off least clearly" (Boatwright, 1961, 29). Ronald Bryden in the *Spectator* praised the story's "insider" quality as well as its style, calling Salter "a poet of his dizzy new element."[13] Most reviewers seemed satisfied with the novel as "a vivid, multifaceted picture of life in the air and on the base."[14]

Nevertheless, *The Arm of Flesh* is the weakest of all Salter's novels. The story is inherently less dramatic than Salter's first, which had a wartime setting. Although landings in fog supply suspense, there are too many of these in the novel. The section that deals with the gunnery meets in North Africa adds diversity and interest, but we see too little of the particulars here to even understand what makes for a hit or a miss and what kinds of pilot skills are involved. The book's largest flaw, however, is its unsuccessful experiment with multivoiced narration. Not only does the technique fail to develop a sustained plot, but the voices themselves are insufficiently unique in inflection and cadence. Is it that pilots flying in the same squadron speak the same language and are equally tight-lipped about personal, emotional issues? Or is it that Salter spreads his speakers so thin that nuances have little room to develop? True, a couple of the speakers, Isbell and Sisse, are more poetic than the others, and in their monologues Salter's writing attains an occasional lyricism. It is also true that all the speakers are convincing in the authenticity of their talk of flying and base life. Ultimately, however, there are just too many speakers, resulting in a lack of differentiation and development, and interrupting the thought progression of the few who matter. As a result, the story has many strains but no true melody. Or to take another analogy, Salter has erected quite a bit of scaffolding but not enough of a building.

Despite, then, its generally firm writing and convincing portrait of American airmen in Europe during the cold war, Salter's ambitious experiment with point of view is a failure, although certainly no disgrace, for its problems result more from overreaching than from lack of talent. Of course, one should remember that seriously flawed novels blemish the early careers of even distinguished writers: Hawthorne had his *Fanshawe*, Melville his *Mardi*, Fitzgerald *The Beautiful and the Damned*, and Sinclair Lewis a whole series of failures before *Main Street*.

## Chapter Three
# Screenwriter *(Downhill Racer, The Appointment, Three, Threshold)*

When the fluent and intelligent Japanese artist in the original edition of Salter's first novel calls film a "crippled art," the hero, Cleve Saville, wonders if it even qualifies as art at all. Since Salter wrote the novel while still in the Air Force in the mid-1950s, the scene suggests that even before he became involved in the film industry he had his doubts about its artistic integrity. Eventually his involvement would include documentary film work as cameraman, writer, and editor, and feature film work as screenwriter and director. Of the many scripts he would write for the screen, four were made into movies: *Downhill Racer* (1968), *The Appointment* (1969), *Three* (1969), and *Threshold* (1983). Then, after more than 10 years of intermittent cinematic involvement, by far the most lucrative period of his writing career, Salter forswore his rough magic, turning away from the invitations and blandishments—the lunches, dinners, and parties—with decisive disdain. In 1982, when his novel *Solo Faces* was published, he had a card printed to facilitate the refusals. It said: "James Salter regrets he is unable to . . ." followed by a list of options (write a screenplay, read a screenplay, direct, etc.) with boxes awaiting the appropriate check. Since then Salter has remained aloof from the film industry. Although he still goes to an occasional movie, his attendance is infrequent and indifferent, like a man going to church without belief.

Salter's first involvement with Hollywood came when he sold the screen rights to *The Hunters* for $60,000 in 1957, shortly after the book was published. With a view toward marshaling the funds to support his writing, he had Paramount structure the payments in four yearly install-ments of $13,000, his share after commissions. After selling the screen rights, Salter had nothing else to do with the film, which starred Robert Mitchum and Robert Wagner. Producer/director Dick Powell and screen-writer Wendell Mayes kept no more than the novel's Korean War situa-tion and its list of characters, gutting the story line in favor of a more conventional Hollywood tale: a love triangle involving Saville

(Mitchum), Lt. Carl Abbot (Lee Phillips), and Abbot's wife (May Britt), who was not even in Salter's story. The movie climaxes in Saville's daring rescue of Abbot after he was downed behind enemy lines, another invention that had no connection with anything in the novel. Lt. Ed Pell (Wagner) retains his cocky attitude, but Hollywood could not allow his brashness to go unchecked as it had in the novel, so Pell gets his comeuppance and learns a lesson of humility from Saville. The movie's aerial footage is impressive, but the story is so trite and so far removed from Salter's original that the author's first brush with Hollywood confirmed his suspicions and left him relieved to have had no part in making the movie.

The money from the sale of the film rights to *The Hunters* allowed Salter time to write *The Arm of Flesh*, which was composed in 1958 and 1959. When that book was finished, he turned his attention to some nonliterary ways of supplementing an income that was needed to support a family of four, which would soon become a family of six with the birth of twins in 1962. One of those ways was the selling of swimming pools. Although he winces at the unpleasantness of the memory and recalls selling only three pools, the job did lead to his fateful meeting with Lane Slate, a television writer who lived not far down the road in Piermont, New York. Impressed by the breadth and independence of Slate's knowledge and by the sureness of his opinions, Salter found a kindred spirit and his needed companion in art and business. Carried along by the wave of enthusiasm for cinematic art then billowing through New York City, the two men began a company to make documentary films. The great European directors like Antonioni, Fellini, and Truffaut were playing in American art theaters, giving hope that new methods could invigorate commercial American cinema.

Salter and Slate's first endeavor, *Daily Life in Ancient Rome,* with a narration from Livy and Sallust, was a commentary about New York, juxtaposing the city's glittering surface with age-old prophetic descriptions of decay. *Daily Life in Ancient Rome* was never finished, but Slate and Salter did make nearly a dozen documentaries. Among their most successful endeavors was the prize-winning *Team Team Team,* a film about college football. Salter played football in high school and has maintained an interest in the game and its legends. I remember once, when our paths happened to cross in Tuscaloosa, Alabama, he was eager to visit the Bear Bryant Museum and was not disappointed by its contents. Even in his late sixties, Salter continued to play touch football in games regularly organized by Peter Matthiessen at his nearby home in Sagaponack, New York.

Slate and Salter also did a 10-part series on the circus for PBS and a film, their final one, on American painters for CBS. The latter focused on 15 contemporary painters such as Andy Warhol (then hardly recognized), Robert Rauschenberg, and Stuart Davis. Since his youth Salter has been a lover of painting and has collected pieces over the years as funds would allow. He continues to sketch, although he brushes away inquiries about this hobby as if they were flies. He would rather talk of Henri Matisse, Pierre Bonnard, Pablo Picasso, Robert Motherwell, or Max Beckman.

Salter's first opportunity to write a feature film came in 1963 at the invitation of Howard Rayfiel, a member of a law firm that specialized in theatrical matters and had Hollywood connections. Rayfiel had secured a director with one film's worth of experience and abundant confidence, and Salter was given a comfortable place to write in a quiet house on Sutton Place that belonged to a friend of the director's. He completed a script called *Goodbye, Bear,* an ode to a "young, irresistibly cynical New York girl, the flower of every generation," as seen through an admirer's eyes. Salter admits the work "would have been better as a poem," and it never made it to celluloid (*BD,* 233). It did attract, however, the attention of a young actor by the name of Robert Redford, who at the time was making a name on the New York stage. Redford somehow came across the script, read it, and invited Salter to lunch. Their pleasant meeting proved the first of many, beginning a string of events that led to Salter's being hired to write a film about ski racing in which Redford would star.

To prepare for the film, after traveling for weeks with the United States ski team, Salter and Redford went to the 1968 Olympics at Grenoble, sleeping in corridors since rooms were unavailable. In his memoir Salter paints the picture of a young and carefree Redford, his life as yet uncomplicated by the pressures of stardom. They discussed the nature of the planned film and the central character that Redford would play. From the start Salter saw the film being about a sports figure who is supremely talented and untouched by humility, cocky, selfish, and outspoken in guarding his own interests. The type has become all too common today, and we have seen its logical extension in the absurdities of baseball players who spit on umpires and basketball players who assault their coaches. Considering that Salter's script was written 30 years ago in a different era with different expectations, it had prophetic overtones. He wrote the story around an idea that survived at least in

one line of dialogue, "the justice of sport." That justice was to be illustrated by the final scene of a jubilant and cocky Redford celebrating his
Olympic victory, his arms raised in triumph, while a little-known young
skier comes slanting down the mountain, besting one by one the
leader's times until he streaks across the line as the surprise Olympic
champion. Needless to say, this was not the way the film would end. A
screenwriter, Salter soon realized, has little say over the final shape of
things. In retrospect he describes the writer's place in the cinematic
process quite memorably: "There is the feeling that directors are dependent on you. In reality they are only attendant, waiting to see what is
brought back, with luck something plump in your jaws. You are at most
a preliminary figure. Their view extends past yours to meetings, cajol-
ings, intrigues. They are the ones who actually create things. How reas-
suring it is to be drawn along by their energy, to linger in their society,
which seems luxurious and perhaps elevated, intimate with that of the
stars themselves" (*BD*, 241). Salter would learn an unforgettable lesson
about film from the experience: writers propose, directors dispose.

*Downhill Racer* (1968) turned out to be an interesting film in a number of ways. Salter's story was original in the unglamorous spin it gave
to the three-year rise of a skiing phenomenon from the other side of the
tracks to the heights of his sport. David Chapplett (Redford) is defined
by his relationships with women, his teammates and coach (Gene Hackman), and the sport itself. The movie begins as Redford is called on to
replace an injured skier on the American team during their winter cam-
paign in Europe. After his first season skiing in Europe, showing
promise but scant success, Redford returns home to Idaho Springs, Colorado, and manages to pick up with his old girlfriend right where he left
off, in the back seat of his father's Chevy, even though he had not both-
ered even to say good-bye to her. When the couple button up and
return to the car's front seat, she tries talking to him about her future,
whether to go to dental school or be a waitress, asking his advice.
Clearly uninterested, Redford replies, "I dunno. You got anymore of that
gum?" Later back in Europe, however, Redford is the one who is
brushed off by a sophisticated beauty (Camilla Sparv) after she has
sported with him for her pleasure and coaxed him into using her boss's
skis for the Olympics. When he bumps into her at a tavern, she pre-
tends all is normal and leads him to her yellow sports car to fetch his
Christmas present. Seated in the front seat, she parries his attempt at a
confrontation with prattle about how busy she has been and other light-
hearted evasions. In the midst of this occurs one of the film's best

moments as Redford reaches over from the passenger seat and leans on the horn until she stops talking. The jarring, defining moment lingers as Sparv silently leaves the car and walks back to the tavern, pausing in front of the door to calmly straighten her hair before joining her friends within. In a sense these parallel but opposite encounters with women illustrate the justice of another kind of sport. Redford toyed with his old flame, but when Sparv reverses the roles, he cannot stand it.

Likewise in his skiing, Redford refuses from the beginning to accept what he considers an affront in the form of low seeding. When he is assigned a start in the 88th position for his first event, he declines to race, claiming there is no point. The tactic works to a degree, for he is moved up to 77th position in his next race. Coach Hackman comments sarcastically, "That's because you skied so well last week." The two clash about respect for the sport, teamwork, and what's required to be a champion. Hackman wins the first round when Redford wipes out in the final race of his first European season, and Hackman dismisses his alibis with a definitive, "You're just not strong enough to win."

Even the middle rounds go to Hackman when he calls down Redford for goading his equally good teammate Creech into a silly race down the course, an unnecessary risk that scares everyone when Creech falls, although he is not injured. In spite of the strength of Hackman's lecture (superbly delivered in a half-sardonic, throwaway manner), the words bounce off Redford's ego like Ping-Pong balls. Creech is made to pay for his foolishness, however, when he falls in his next race and is so badly hurt that he is out of the Olympics. As the big event nears and Hackman realizes that Redford is his only hope for a medal, the coach becomes a cheerleader despite his dislike for Redford's attitude. In the end, when Redford electrifies the crowd by blowing past the times of all the major European challengers, Hackman is right there celebrating with him. He is raising Redford's arms when he suddenly notices that an unknown Austrian is streaking down the mountain with even faster intervals. A hush creeps over the crowd. Here is where the film veers from Salter's original script, however, for the young skier crashes, allowing the Americans to return to their celebration. The only glimmer of Redford's vulnerability comes in the look he exchanges with the unknown as the latter picks himself up and slides by.

The film was widely praised. Pauline Kael liked its freshness of feeling and tempo and its sense of freedom, although she did not care for the laconic nature of Salter's script and the story's lack of comment on what it means to the Redford character to become a champion or "what it is in him that makes him one."[1] Knowing Salter's original conception, we can see why the film might leave one unenlightened and unsatisfied. Redford was the wrong actor for the role of the raw outsider with talent and attitude. He embodies the latter two qualities just fine, but he never seems an outsider, projecting too much of the aura of a golden boy for the audience to ever believe he came from that derelict farm in Idaho Springs or was sired by a troll-like father, who looks more like his grandfather. The problem is not, as Kael suggests, the inarticulateness of the Redford character or the film's lack of insight about what makes a champion, for we know by now that great athletes generally have nothing to say because they know no secret to their prowess. Moreover, we do understand why Redford wins in the film: he is gifted and he is daring. The real problem with the film is its moral weakening. It grew ambiguous about its brattish hero, seduced perhaps by the personality of Redford himself, his charm and winning aura. It is especially disconcerting to observe Hackman as coach fawning over the spoiled and celebrated winner. Had the hero been dealt his defeat, it would have unified the film by conveying a sense of the rough justice of sport, which Salter originally had in mind.

A number of film projects and film people occupied Salter's attention in the 1960s even though he found time to write perhaps his finest novel, *A Sport and a Pastime,* in the midst of it all. One of his first undertakings was an Italian story of love and jealousy, commissioned by director Peter Glenville, which drew Salter to Rome for months in 1963 and 1964, where he found entry into the knowing life of old Europe and met such figures as Fellini and Zavattini. The latter, who wrote the films *The Bicycle Thief* and *Umberto D.,* told Salter that the film industry had failed, that it never achieved the promises of a "new, fresh, politically meaningful art" (*BD,* 251). The time in Italy served as a kind of novitiate, introducing Salter to the sophisticated, sybaritic ways of Europe's cognoscenti. One door opened onto another, and behind each lay stories, most about desires and their fulfillment, like the story of Pietro Germi, "who left his wife for a young actress and had been betrayed by her in a most humiliating way" (*BD,* 248–49), or that of the famous actress who liked to make love two ways at the same time. An Italian singer and actress told Salter that he should set his film in Bologna, not Rome, for Bologna was famous for three things: its learning, its food, and its fellatio (*BD,* 244). "We were in the ancient world," Salter comments about the dinner party that night, "in the cool air, the darkness beneath the vines" (*BD,* 243).

In this ancient world, by chance one evening at a restaurant, Salter met a striking beauty, who happened to be the mistress of John Huston, then shooting scenes for *The Bible* in Rome. Huston was a legendary womanizer, who in his autobiography listed the names of more than a dozen women who were his lovers besides his five wives. Thinking of them, he said he was "like a pirate counting spoils at the end of a long voyage."[2] Before long Salter was reading this beautiful 23-year-old's palm, and in the course of things he too became part of her love line. "Ilena," as Salter calls her in his memoir, had previously been the companion of Farouk, the late king of Egypt. When Salter met Ilena, she was being supported by an Italian businessman as well as by Huston, and she was married, for the sake of obtaining a passport, to an 80-year-old man confined to a home for the elderly. Salter accepted Ilena as an exotic gift from the old world and did not complicate their interlude together with feelings of jealousy or ambitions of possession.

Ironically the script that Salter was then writing hinged on jealousy as the main cause of the tragedy. Perhaps its plot served as a caution to himself. The finished movie was called *The Appointment* (1969), directed by Sidney Lumet and starring Omar Sharif and Anouk Aimee. Salter is hard on all aspects of the film, which somehow made its way to Cannes as the American entry. He says that Lumet, despite his reputation, was ill-suited for the project, taking it on only because he wanted the opportunity to learn something about color photography from the experienced Italian cinematographer Carlo Di Palma. Indeed, there are moments during the film when the camera seems to grow bored with the action and assumes a mind of its own, lingering interminably on panoramic shots. Lumet in his autobiography confirms Salter's account, admitting that the only reason he did the film was to learn effective use of color from Di Palma, who had shot *The Red Desert* for Antonioni. Lumet says that Salter's dialogue was "fine," but the "dreadful story line that had been handed to him by an Italian producer" did the film in.[3] Lumet makes no comment on the stars, who Salter felt were badly miscast: Sharif as the passionate young lawyer who wins Aimee after she is dumped by a business acquaintance, then grows suspicious of her character; Aimee as the wife suspected of high-priced prostitution who is driven to depression, despair, and finally suicide. As for his own script, Salter says it was unsuited for Lumet, and it "should have been ripped at the seams and completely refashioned to make it fit" (*BD*, 269). His fondest memory of making the film is chatting between takes with Lotte Lenya, who played a small but effective role as a procuress for the well heeled. When the film was screened at Cannes, Salter recalls the audience breaking into laughter at a moment of solemn seriousness.

Indeed, *The Appointment* is seriously flawed, although not without interest. The whole fulcrum of Sharif's moonstruck pursuit of Aimee is a chance love-at-first-sighting of her walking along a narrow street. Sharif's love is packaged in suspicion, however, after he is given evidence that she occasionally sells herself for enormous sums. His character is so blocked emotionally, so unable to express either love or doubt, that the principal effect on the audience is frustration. Likewise the story withholds the mysterious source of Aimee's pain from both Sharif and the audience. The film's finale, when Sharif's doubts are dispelled too late, is moving, but it does not bring us any enlightenment on Aimee's suicide, nor is it conclusive about her suspect life. As the lawyer portrayed by Sharif walks out of his office crushed by the irony of his false suspicions, he cuts a pathetic figure who has been deformed by jealousy and must suffer its results. This is insufficient reward for a film that hinted at other, more interesting, complexities by dropping clues that Sharif may have been attracted, albeit unconsciously, to Aimee *because* of her suspected wildness. After all, Sharif had gone to the specialty procuress independent of his interest in Aimee, buying the services of a schoolgirl, and there were hints that he may have been even disappointed on one level by not having his suspicions about Aimee confirmed. Despite echoes of Antonioni, *The Appointment* ultimately failed to engage its viewers in the tragic emotions of the love story, for the story shed no sustained enlightenment on the underlying motivations of its principals.

With money from various film projects, in early autumn of 1967 Salter took his wife and four children to Europe to spend the year living in southern France and writing. They sailed in first-class cabins on the *France,* enjoying the amenities with fellow travelers Edward Albee and Madeleine Carroll. They lived in Magagnosc, a village near Grasse, renting an old three-story farmhouse with a commanding view of the sea from three sides and of mountains from the fourth. The house was called *La Moutonne,* and it had been occupied the previous year by Eleanor Clark and Robert Penn Warren. Clark had written to Salter, when he inquired about the place, that it would be "the most wonderful year of your life if you don't freeze to death," for the house was unheated. He describes the inconvenience vividly: "In the worst months of winter the sheets were so cold we could not turn over in bed—we lay like statues of saints, rigid, arms crossed" (*BD,* 263). Fortunately fall was long, winter short, and the family was able to spend many sun-drenched days on the sands of the nearby Mediterranean. Despite the house being named for a female sheep, its resident farm animal was a white goat, Lily, who roamed free during the day and was kept in a shed at night. Salter liked the goat's unaffectionate independence, and she was a favorite with his children as she had been with the Warrens' children the year before. Occasionally she would climb the shed's red tile roof and step onto the balcony where Salter was writing at a worn wooden table. With the goat and the house's other charms—its quiet seclusion, wild gardens, terraces, plentiful olive trees, views, and nearness to the sea—the year was indeed wonderful, at least until May, when an illness in the family clouded life. A boil appeared overnight in the nose of Salter's 11-year-old daughter Nina, spreading such virulent infection that her life actually hung in the balance. She survived and recovered, but the event turned out to be a kind of foreshadowing, like the ploy of a novelist to prepare one for oncoming disaster, for 12 years later Nina's sister Allan died in a freak electrical accident in the shower. Salter writes in his memoir: "Even if the rest get through, there is always the thought of that one" (*BD*, 268).

By some coincidence the films Salter had been writing all went into production within a year of one another. *Downhill Racer* was released in 1968, *The Appointment* in 1969, and his last and most ambitious venture, *Three*, also in 1969. The latter was based on Irwin Shaw's story "Then We Were Three," and, with Shaw's blessing, Salter assumed the role of director as well as writer. Some time before, Shaw had entertained thoughts of writing a script for the story himself, but he turned instead to another of his stories, "In the French Style," which he brought to the screen as both writer and producer. Shaw's film, starring Jean Seberg as the young American girl in Paris, was treated unkindly by most reviewers, but it was savaged by *Time*.[4]

*Three* involves two young American friends (Sam Waterston and Robie Porter) traveling in Europe and meeting a girl (Charlotte Rampling), American in the original but English in the film, also on holiday. The three become a unit and even make a pact to preserve their friendship by curtailing any romantic inclinations within the triad. When Porter gets briefly involved with another girl they encounter in their travels, Waterston realizes just how strongly he is attached to Rampling, even fantasizing a proposal of marriage after their holiday is over and their pact expired. With difficulty he keeps his feelings to himself. When Porter returns from his fling, however, he is not so scrupulous, immediately having an affair with Rampling that leads to a break between the two old friends. Waterston returns to the States, leaving the pair to their own devices, everyone saddened but wiser.

The film won praise at Cannes, got many good reviews in the United States, and even made it to some critics' top 10 lists. Its supporters found it charming, natural, and praised the director's light-handed subtlety. But perhaps it was a trifle too subtle, for it never attracted much of an audience and has since been allowed to disappear without a trace. Salter himself can only muster up enough enthusiasm for his sole writing/directing venture to call it "decorous and mildly attractive" (*BD*, 272). In retrospect, he admits he was "too restrained, to mention only one shortcoming, in both the scenes I wrote and the direction that I gave the actors" (*BD*, 270). Moreover, he had all sorts of trouble with his leading lady, who he says was frequently and unapologetically late, short-tempered, and mean—everything a star is supposed to be. Of course, the coup de grâce came when, halfway through the filming, she refused to continue unless her salary was doubled and her boyfriend replaced Salter as director. Rampling ended up compromising for half of her demands, and the shoot was completed. Salter now wonders if the finished product might have been better had the boyfriend actually taken over and "made of the well-behaved film something crude but poignant—that is to say compelling" (*BD*, 271).

The completed film was honored by judges but ignored by the public. It also caused a chill in Salter's relationship with Shaw, who detested it as a travesty of his story (Shnayerson, 271). The strain was temporary, and Shaw eventually resolved his disappointment under the rationale that Salter was a lyric writer, while he was a narrative one (*BD*, 210). The whole experience cured Salter of his directorial impulse. Never again would he direct another film, although there were opportunities. He knew that such work was taking him far from his *moyen*, reminding himself that "it was Céline I liked, Cavafy" (*BD*, 273). But it would still be some time before he abandoned film altogether, for he was fascinated by the extravagance of it all, the first-class transatlantic flights during which stewardesses roamed the aisles with platters of roast carved to order, the impulsive boat trips to Torcello for lunch, "jolting across the wide lagoon, the wind blowing the dark green water to whiteness." At the time, Salter admits, it was not so easy to distinguish "the real and the false glory" (*BD*, 272). No doubt the money was part of the attraction, for screenwriters are paid well whether their scripts reach the screen or not. Once, when Salter was leaving to research a project in

Europe, the producer handed him a wad of traveler's checks "for inci-
dentals" (*BD,* 274). This particular project, whose producer, Robert
Emmett Ginna, became one of Salter's closest friends, depended like
most film undertakings on attracting an important director and famous
stars to ensure studio backing. At one time Salter and Ginna had
elicited a commitment from Paul Scofield based on the condition they
enlist the services of either Maggie Smith, Vanessa Redgrave, or Ingrid
Bergman. One by one the women turned them down, and the film was
never made. Salter now regards such losses with stoic indifference, probably because he has canceled all such entries from the ledger of his art.
In fact, he seems perfectly willing to consign to a common burial plot
his unfilmed scripts and those that became celluloid. He is not so cava-
lier about the film writing of others and asserts that "the best scripts are
not always made, just as the hardest fought campaigns may not end in
victory" (*BD,* 282). As proof he cites the example of Robert Bolt, one of
the screen's most successful writers, whose version of the *Bounty* mutiny,
Salter avers, is the best script he ever read, "a work of high ambition"
(*BD,* 286–87). It was never filmed.

Even while working on his own fiction, Salter continued to bob in
"the floating world" of film throughout the 1970s. In the early part of
the decade, he joined forces with Christopher Mankiewicz, the famous
director's son, writing a script called *Raincoat,* which went the typical
promising course: a studio interested, a major actor committed, much of
the financing in place; then came the typical glitches: studio wants a
rewrite, actor departs for a more appealing project, they scramble for a
new star, and the uneventful months pass into inactivity and finally
abandonment.

One more of Salter's scripts, however, did get filmed. *Threshold*
(1983) was made in Canada and did not have its U.S. release until two
years after its Canadian. It deals with heart transplant surgery, specifi-
cally with the pioneering use of an artificial heart, a subject that Salter
had written a long article about for *Life* (September 1981). Donald
Sutherland is masterful as the brilliant, commanding, and dedicated surgeon, Dr. Thomas Vrain, who connects emotionally with his patients,
and Jeff Goldblum is effective as the nerdy visionary, Dr. Aldo Gehring,
whose iconoclastic ideas sweep aside all other considerations. The pair-
ing of the two in a quest to make a medical breakthrough gives the film
momentum and suspense. While Gehring designs and tests his artificial
devices in animals, Vrain continues his routine heroisms of daily bypass
surgeries and heart transplants, with the victories and defeats in one

area nicely counterpointing those in the other. The two tensions coalesce when Gehring succeeds in his animal experimentation at about the same time that Vrain encounters a former patient whose deteriorating heart suggests drastic measures. When conventional surgery on Carol Severance (Mare Winningham) fails and she is at the point of death on Vrain's operating table, Vrain turns to Gehring and asks, "Where is that thing?" Severance's artificial heart implant is accomplished, and her physical condition improves nicely after the operation. The only problem is that she refuses to talk. Meanwhile, Gehring is swept up into the postoperative acclaim, and Vrain is unable to rein in his accomplice's crowing and metaphysical rambling before the media. In the midst of a radio interview, Gehring undercuts Vrain's role in the breakthrough by pontificating: "Surgery is only repetition. It's just plumbing. It has no intellectual aspects." This posturing is immediately followed by a wonderful scene of Vrain patiently sitting with Carol and finally succeeding in getting her to talk, airing her deep misgivings about her condition. In drawing out Carol's feelings of fear (that the device will just stop working) and doubt (that she is fully human now that a machine controls her body), Vrain is shown to be a true hero, as skilled in understanding the human heart as operating on it.

The film is well paced, with riveting photography of open-heart surgery alternating with scenes of backstage hospital politics, Vrain's family life, and the daily patient traumas. A quiet moment at a cocktail party early in the film explains the implications of the title. A journalist compares Los Angeles, where the story takes place, to Florence during an era when money, art, and science were all joined together, suggesting that Los Angeles is a city at the end of one era of American expansion and at the beginning of another. The idea of uncharted territory is the movie's dominant metaphor, although it is Vrain's heroism that leaves the strongest impression, for in him we see the surgeon as savior as well as pioneer. The journalist's comments prepare the audience for this emphasis when he says: "People come here because you [Vrain] are the best. People come here when they've been given up for dead. They come here expecting miracles."

The dialogue is sharp and convincing throughout, although its author, characteristically self-critical, points only to shortcomings: "The writing, as one sees often in retrospect, was imperfect, but I could not at the time imagine how to improve it. The budget was too small and the actors were not all ones we wanted. Some of the best scenes were dropped or awkwardly played as a result. . . . When I finally saw the movie, feeling as always naked in the audience, I saw mostly the flaws, quite a few of them my own" (*BD*, 299).

One can see why Salter was attracted to the subject matter of the film, for heroism has always fascinated him, and this is the heroism of medicine at its most daring and exploratory edge. Thresholds, like that of the first man to go to the moon or that of the first artificial heart implant, are important stuff, and the pioneers are true heroes. Despite Salter's misgivings about the movie, it does convey how the combination of genius and commitment, when given the resources, can lead to such breakthroughs. The movie also reveals the uncertainty about what awaits us on the other side of the portal, for who knows if initial success will lead to ultimate success, and who knows what the human effects of such success will be.

Salter wrote other scripts, but none of these became films. His novel *Solo Faces* was originally a screenplay commissioned by Robert Redford, but Redford did not care for the finished product. It too might have gone the way of Salter's other ghost scripts but for the proposal from Robert Emmett Ginna, then managing editor at Little, Brown, that Salter turn the story into a novel. After that book was published, Salter had his "James Salter regrets he is unable to . . ." card printed to facilitate his turning down all movie offers. He did relent, however, and agree to write in the mid-1980s what was intended to be a final screenplay about an interview granted by a reclusive movie star to a writer. They fall in love, the star with everything and the writer with nothing but his knowledge of the past. Salter muses: "Perhaps I dreamed I was the writer and the irresistible woman who had not, for years, had the least whim denied her was a symbol for film itself" (*BD*, 301). Perhaps, but the film industry did not fall in love with Salter, and neither that script nor still another that he relented and wrote, now truly his last, was made. Offers continued to drift his way, but the realization that had come years before, that this was not the life for him, needed finally to be acted on before it was too late. As Salter explains, "At a certain point one stands on the isthmus and sees clearly the Atlantic and Pacific of life. There is the destiny of going one way or the other and you must choose. And so the phantom, which in truth I was, passed from sight" (*BD*, 301).

It is no wonder that Salter now deflects inquiries about his films and film connections with a dismissive comment about their insignificance. The glitter of Hollywood and its stars of the moment continue to fascinate our public consciousness, such that when Salter gives readings or even classes in writing, the questions inevitably cluster around the movies. He understands. After all, wasn't he one of the moths who fluttered around the lights for more than a decade? And yet, as Cheever had said of another kind of life, "That person in the army, that wasn't me," so Salter has realized about himself and the life of making films, "that wasn't me." All that remains now of those days is "a kind of silky pollen that clings to the fingertips and brings back what was once pleasurable—too pleasurable, perhaps—the lights dancing on dark water as in the old prints, the sound of voices, laughter, music, all faint, alluring, far off" (*BD,* 304).

## Chapter Four

# The Indelible Book
# (*A Sport and a Pastime*)

No book by Salter has been praised more highly than *A Sport and a Pastime*. Reynolds Price has said that the novel "is as nearly perfect as any American fiction I know" (Price, 3). *Esquire,* to which Salter has been a frequent contributor, called it "one of the great literary works of our day" (Editorial Note, 101). Salter himself, notoriously self-critical, believed in the book from the start despite its rejection by his own publisher, Harper Brothers, who commented that it was too repetitive and uninteresting and that the characters were too unsympathetic. Other rejections followed before a friend of the author showed the manuscript to George Plimpton, editor of the *Paris Review,* who instantly accepted it for his new Paris Review Editions, an imprint published by Doubleday. Although the Paris Review Editions had been committed to "making no compromise with the public taste," Doubleday was never comfortable with the *A Sport and a Pastime*'s eroticism and treated the book as awkwardly as the company's founder, Frank Doubleday, had treated Dreiser's great and scandalous *Sister Carrie* at the turn of the century. Salter's book sold only a few thousand copies in this 1967 edition, and it was not until North Point Press reissued it in 1985 that the novel began to reach a somewhat wider audience, although its continued life has always depended more on a small number of fervent admirers, many of them writers, than on the masses. These admirers were vindicated a decade later when *A Sport and a Pastime* was added to the list of distinguished classics selected for the Modern Library imprint.

In the autumn of 1966, after the novel had been written but before it appeared in print, Salter sensed he had come close to his exalted ambition of writing "an immaculate book filled with images of an unchaste world more desirable than our own, a book which would cling to one and could not be brushed away" (*BD,* 316). Truman Capote's *In Cold Blood* had just been published, filling Salter with envy "for its exceptional clarity and power," and that November Capote gave a spectacular party at the Plaza to celebrate. The guest list included writers, artists, movie stars, tycoons, princesses, and statesmen, but since he knew neither Capote nor his guests, it did not include Salter, who was driving by the Plaza that evening as many of the party "were going up the carpeted steps of the hotel entrance." Salter recalls feeling elated in his solitude, scorning the glitter, emboldened by the promise of his own creation, the manuscript that lay "deep in my pocket, like an inheritance" (*BD,* 318).

Salter wrote most of *A Sport and a Pastime* between 1964 and 1966 in an apartment on Downing Street in Greenwich Village, a working studio that he shared with Ed Nielsen, who had edited *Three* and Salter's documentaries on the circus. Like the other suburban commuters who pour into the city in the morning, work, and are out again by evening, Salter made the daily trip to his studio, where he spun an unconventional tale of travel and desire that is the antithesis of quotidian responsibilities. With a confidence and aspiration hardly justified by his previous two novels, Salter felt the time had come to show what he could do. He wanted to create something at once pure and licentious, "to describe things that were unspeakable in one sense, but at the same time, irresistible" ("Art," 77)—the kind of forbidden perfection of an opium dream, intense but inexpressible. He wrote, at times in a trancelike fervor, as if copying a novel that had already been composed in his mind. Three years before, he had spent a year in France when recalled to active Air Force duty during the 1961 Berlin crisis. While stationed in Chaumont, a town squarely in the midst of the French provinces about three hours from Paris, he met a young French girl, "innocent in her beauty," and traveled the countryside with her, exploring towns and their architecture (*BD,* 344). Occasionally he jotted down things seen and done, and these notes became the basis for his novel, supplying experiential grounding to his story, giving it a voice of assurance and authenticity. Salter had been smitten by France before this stay, his first visit occurring in 1950, and he would return many times throughout his life, but no visit enamored him more of the country than that of 1961: "Almost everything I feel and cherish about France came from that year—the vintage for me of the century, one might say."[1] In a coda to 1961, Salter tells in his memoir of meeting the real-life counterpart of *A Sport and a Pastime*'s Anne-Marie Costallat at Kennedy airport when she first arrived in America. Eventually, he reports, she married, had children, and settled in Los Angeles. "It was," says Salter, "very like the book" (*BD,* 344).

## Journeys

*A Sport and a Pastime* begins as a travel narrative, and the exploration of foreign places is the thread that connects every element of the story, its characters, style, events, and themes. The novel is Salter's hymn to "green, bourgeois France" (*SP,* 4). Through the wanderings of a young American man and a younger, small-town French girl, the novel reveals the country's "secret life . . . into which one cannot penetrate, the life of photograph albums, uncles, names of dogs that have died" (*SP,* 4). France would be inaccessible, remote, and lifeless to Phillip Dean without his affair with the beautiful, though cheap, Anne-Marie Costallat. She becomes the other, the person who illuminates travel, whom one always dreams of meeting, and without whom the museums grow tedious, the roads empty, and the restaurants a necessity. Anne-Marie provides Dean, 24 and a dropout from Yale, with a personal reference, hence perspective, rescuing him from the lost ranks of student sightseers. Architecture, mountains, great rivers, and villages must have a scale, one that is emotional as well as historical and numerical.

The story's unnamed narrator, older than Dean but still young at 30, is also on holiday in France, and it is he who first sets an agenda devoted to travel: "I am going to walk these village roads, follow these brilliant streams" (*SP,* 6). The book begins with his leaving Paris by train for the provinces, and this initial journey establishes the paradigm for his and Dean's subsequent peregrinations. Movement, places, people. Three times within the space of two pages this pattern is repeated: "We are going at tremendous speed. . . . The farms are built of stone. . . .She [a girl on the train] has moles on her face, too, and one of her fingers is bandaged. I try to imagine where she works—a *patisserie,* I decide" (*SP,* 4). Each time the same order is followed: "We seem to be going faster. . . . Cesson, a pale station with an old clock. . . . Across from me the girl has fallen asleep" (*SP,* 4–5). Travel's ultimate goal is knowledge, *connaisance,* to become familiar with that which was foreign, to appropriate the new and make it one's own. But such knowledge, it is revealed, is empty, futile without a personal connection. If that connection is denied in fact, it can be created through the imagination, the power of entering into the life of another through observation and deduction. The narrator illustrates this when, after the girl with the mole departs the train, his eye alights on another: "a silent girl with a face like a bird, one of those hard little faces, the bones close beneath. A passionate face. The face of a

girl who might move to the city. . . . Around her neck is a band of imitation diamonds. It seems I am seeing everything more clearly. The details
of a whole world are being opened to me" (*SP,* 6–7). The discovery of
the salient fact, the band of imitation diamonds around her neck,
becomes the detail that reveals the personal, allowing him to imagine
the girl's life. Suddenly everything else around him, the landscape and
the towns, is illuminated.

Because he is a photographer, the narrator's eye is practiced at spot-
ting such seemingly insignificant personal details that illuminate the
places visited. In fact, he asks us to read his narration as "notes to photographs of Autun," although, as he admits, it could be Auxerre or any
of the small towns at the heart of France whose essence he dreams of
capturing with his lens. His exemplar is the famous Atget, who created
"great voiceless images" of Paris, "stealing a city from those who inhab-
ited it, a tree here, a store front, an immortal fountain" (*SP,* 13). Of
course, the photographer does not appear in his own photographs, and
it is not *his* experience of the personal that is destined to illuminate the
provincial places. His glancing at the girls on the train and later others
(he, in fact, notices Anne-Marie before Dean does) exhibits his desire,
which he realizes is an instrument of navigation, but desire without rec-
iprocation remains sterile. Despite his longing for the widow, Claude
Picquet, and for Anne-Marie, he never achieves intimacy, except
through his imaginative entry into the lives of others. For the total experience of travel, the photographer/narrator must picture the emprises of
Phillip Dean, who had been touring Spain before being introduced to
the narrator by mutual friends in Paris. Dean comes to visit him in
Autun in September, intending a stay of only days, and he does not
leave until the beginning of summer.

## Journeys and Intimations of Journeys

Like another American who extended his excursion abroad, Chad New-
some of Henry James's *The Ambassadors,* Phillip Dean discovers the
deeper and darker life of Europe through intimacy with a woman.
Madame de Vionnet epitomized Parisian nobility as fully as Anne-Marie
Costallat embodies the commonness of the French provinces. The sexual
dimension, essential though veiled in James, is both crucial and open
here. Dean comes to know "the secret life of France, into which one cannot penetrate" through his penetration of Anne-Marie (*SP,* 4). His penis
enters her *penus* (Latin for house), and the narrator, with the breathless

gaze of a voyeur, uses his instrument (camera/pen) to record the posses-sion, the process of naturalization. Passages of lovemaking alternate with passages of travel. Sex becomes both a means to and an analogy of the discovery of place. Anne-Marie, Dean's guide, translator, compan-ion, and the emotional measure of his adventure in a foreign land, is also his mistress, and the contours and texture of her body signify for him the physical nature of the countryside itself. France accepts Dean when Anne-Marie takes him into her arms. Nowhere has it been made clearer that travel is a sensuous experience—all sights, smell, tastes, sounds, and touches. Dean's exploration of Anne-Marie, as common and lovely as the French provinces, becomes an *explication du texte* of the country itself. Her body is cathedral and cave, restaurant and marketplace, courtyard and cheap hotel. After they have made love for the first time, "she falls asleep without a word. Dean lies beside her. The real France, he is thinking. The real France. He is lost in it, in the smell of the very sheets" (*SP,* 53–54).

Dean's triumph in the novel is that he comes to know France through his knowledge of Anne-Marie, revealing just how analogous and recip-rocal are the experiences of travel and sex, the exotic and the erotic. On the elemental level, travel is defined by entry into the territory of another just as in sex one invades the space, the privacy of another's body, giving sexual contact its adventure. Of course, the safest thing in the world is to stay at home, just as abstention from sex is the safest way to ensure one's physical, emotional, and moral integrity. As for the lat-ter, the amorphous but instinctive taboo surrounding sex is the first vio-lation that lovers make. For Dean and Anne-Marie this occurs in a Paris hotel after they have showered together: "He has wrapped her in an enormous towel, soft as a robe, and carried her to the bed. They lie across it diagonally, and he begins to draw the towel apart with care, to remove it as if it were a bandage. Her flesh appears, still smelling a little of soap. His hands float onto her. The sum of small acts begins to unite them, the pure calculus of love. He feels himself enter. Her last breath—it is almost a sigh—leaves her. Her white throat appears" (*SP,* 52). Apparitions like Anne-Marie's white throat reward the pilgrim's visitation of the grotto of love, and in the altered light of their intimacy the fountains and the town squares appear wondrous and familiar.

More startling visions await further encroachments. In travel one delights in the discovery of the new, the trespassing upon unfamiliar ter-ritory. So in sex. In travel this pleasure is compounded when the unveil-ing is not normally allowed. So in sex. What could be more satisfying, more thrilling than visiting a shrine, a castle, a private collection to which the public is forbidden? So in *A Sport and a Pastime,* the sexual encounters are charged by their flagrancy and by their gradual movement toward foreign, even forbidden, ground. The violation of each taboo carries Dean into a deeper intimacy with the life around him, his "first innocence changed into long Sunday mornings, the bells filling the air, pillows jammed under her belly, her marvelous behind high in the daylight" (*SP,* 57). There is something illicit, obsessive, about this affair, raising images we repudiate until they are transformed by the apparition of the experience itself into a world more immaculate, more innocent, than our own.

Salter's style is crucial in this process, and he gambles everything on it, making the lovers' travels the book's aria and their sexual encounters its recitative. In each town visited, the special qualities of that place are sung in reverent cadences:

> Sens. The famous cathedral which is reflected in the splendor of Canterbury itself rises over the icy river, over the still streets. One sees it in the distance, St. Etienne: the centuries have bleached its stone like powder and the heads are all missing from statues of the blessed, but still it appears from far off to warn travelers of the presence of God. Built as one of the first of a great, Gothic family that rose throughout France, it endures like a white myth. The little shops have grown close around it, cinemas, restaurants. Still, it cannot be touched. Beneath the noon sun the roof, which is typically Burgundian, gleams in the strange design of snakeskin, banded into diamonds, black and green, ocher, red. The sun splashes it like water. The brilliance seems to spread. (*SP,* 84)

The majesty and historic weight of the places seen lend a dignity to Dean and Anne-Marie's journeys and hence to the sightseers themselves. Here it is the cathedral of St. Etienne in its bleached brilliance. Salter's descriptions are monuments for contemplation, first riveting the reader on the objects themselves, which travel writing often does not do in its impatience to tell *about* the places. Homely details like the snakeskin pattern of the roof are juxtaposed with a register of the cathedral's emotional impact as both a victim and a survivor of time's destructiveness. Besides enabling the reader to contemplate the scene and feel its power, however, Salter's description also creates an aura of sanctity and mystery that suffuses and colors Dean and Anne-Marie's sacred rites. The apparition of the "white myth" of the cathedral recalls the earlier apparition of Anne-Marie's "white throat." That too is mythical and pure.

Without losing the realism of the couple's sexual encounters, their bold effrontery, Salter's language captures their splendor as well as their melodic variations: "With a touch like flowers, she is gently tracing the base of his cock, driven now all the way into her, touching his balls, and beginning to writhe slowly beneath him in a sort of obedient rebellion while in his own dream he rises a little and defines the moist rim of her cunt with his finger, and as he does, he comes like a bull" (*SP*, 58). The shock of "cock," "balls" and "cunt" is interwoven with the romance of "flowers" and "dream" and the realism of "writhe" and "moist rim." The paradox of "obedient rebellion" describes her response to his entry, obedient because she is below him doing what he wants, but rebellious in her aggressive writhing, her counterinsurgency that seeks her own pleasure. Dean talks to Anne-Marie about "all the ways to love, the sweet variety," and she is eager. Together they explore this variety in scenes of searing sensuality, their sexual adventure paralleling their exploration of town after French town: Nancy, Sens, Avallon, Besancon, Dole, Angers.

They discard inhibition after inhibition, coming at last to the violation Dean has been craving, anal sex. When he asks her afterward if she liked it, she answers, "Beaucoup." It is the signal that all barriers are down and they have come into complete possession of each other: "A feast of love is beginning. Everything that has gone before is only a sort of introduction. Now they are lovers. The first, wild courses are ended. They have founded their domain" (*SP*, 109). The territorial metaphor indicates that they are no longer sightseers or travelers but have laid claim to the French provinces as surely as they have laid claim to one another. We are disarmed by the gratuitousness and totality of their sexual love, hypnotized by the reverent cadences of Salter's prose, and overwhelmed by the beauty of their transformation, observing Dean's passage from stranger to king, now in full possession of his kingdom, the territory he has invaded: "Mythology has accepted him. . . . He tumbles into the damp leaves of love, he rises clean as air" (*SP*, 76). Both Dean and the cathedral are part of the realm of myth. Both are physically immediate, the cathedral's phallic quality mirroring Dean's condition. Dean becomes one with Anne-Marie, one with France. The novel thus celebrates the twin glories of sexual love and place as they are revealed to be analogous experiences. After Dean has confided the details of his sorties to the narrator, the latter thinks: "Somehow I have the impression that he is laying it all before me, the essence of this glorious life he has spent in France" (*SP*, 163).

## Not for Everyone: The Narrator

Two qualifying revelations about "this glorious life" are contained in the novel: it is not accessible to everyone, and it will not last. The first idea is communicated through the novel's narrator, its self-dubbed "agent provocateur." Salter in interviews has said that he intended the narrator to have no particular significance. He rejected an objective third-person narration, for he felt it "would be a little disturbing because of the explicitness, the sexual descriptions" ("Art," 79). On the other hand, having Dean relate his own escapades would result in awkwardness and self-absorption. He hit on the idea instead of having someone not important to the action serve as "intermediary between the book and the reader" ("Art," 79). As for the first-person spectator he created, Salter admits, "You could say it's me; well, possibly. But truly, there is no such person. He's a device. He's like the figure in black that moves the furniture in a play, so to speak, essential, but not part of the action" ("Art," 79). The difference, of course, is that in plays the figure in black normally does not talk to the audience. When he does, as say in the case of the Common Man in Robert Bolt's *A Man for All Seasons,* he becomes an important part of the drama.

Despite Salter's disavowal of any postmodernist intentions, it is hard to read the narrator's frequent admissions of his own untrustworthiness without seeing the work in the light of postmodernist fiction: "I am not telling the truth about Dean," he avers. "I am inventing him. I am creating him out of my own inadequacies, you must always remember that" (*SP,* 76). Because of such undercutting of his own reliability, the narrator, one reviewer claimed, "is the only personality one can study" in the novel,[2] a sentiment that is echoed by Margaret Winchell Miller, who claims: "The narrator is a magician; the story he has related is not a real story at all, but a product of his self-conscious imagination" (Miller, 5). I agree that the narrator is more than Salter makes him out to be, that he is a fascinating character worthy of our attention. Both reviewer and critic, however, go too far in the amount of credence they give to the narrator's disclaimer, which should be balanced by the overwhelmingly realistic detail with which he describes the story of Anne-Marie and Dean. It is true that the narrator has been interposed between the reader and the action, but not magically imposed as Winchell suggests. The narrator observes carefully, and he admits that Dean has confided in him up to a point. Beyond that point, he may rely on his imagination, but the imagination is sure, for he is at one with Dean in their desire for Anne-Marie.

The narrator serves as the reader's filter and guide, but one never gets the impression that he is capricious or misleading despite his disclaimer, which strikes one like the note at the beginning of novels, "This tale has no resemblance to anyone living or dead." Sure. The descriptions of Dean's times with Anne-Marie, the details of their preparations and departures are too specific, too authentic to be diminished by the narrator's disclaimer. Moreover, the truth that the narrator is seeking is the truth of experience rather than the truth of a hidden camera. Nowhere is his voice more sincere in the novel than when he says, "Certain things I remember exactly as they were. They are merely discolored a bit by time, like coins in the pocket of a forgotten suit. Most of the details, though, have long since been transformed or rearranged to bring others of them forward. Some, in fact, are obviously counterfeit; they are no less important. One alters the past to form the future. But there is a real significance to the pattern which finally appears, which resists all further change" (*SP*, 46). Forget the isolated detail. On the level of experience, it is as impossible to doubt the narrator's account of Dean and Anne-Marie as it would be to discount a criminal confession that fits every clue of the crime but that the confessed now disclaims.

The narrative technique, then, does not decrease the reality of Dean as much as it increases the reality of the narrator, sharpening the reader's perception that, like the narrator, "One must have heroes, which is to say, one must create them" (*SP*, 180). The inadequacies of the narrator, out of which he admits to be partially inventing Dean, express an essential longing of human beings for the ineffable, in this case Dean's "power which I cannot identify, which is flickering . . . this power which guarantees his existence, ever afterwards, even when he is gone" (*SP*, 167). We must not forget that this was to be a *wanderjahr* for the narrator himself, ripe with the hope of fulfilling his own erotic and pastoral longings. Cristina in Paris, Madame Picquet, and Anne-Marie herself all slip past the scope of his desire. Of the latter, he insists, "It was by glances, exhausted glances across a nightclub that I discovered her, and I confirmed her only in silence, in stealth . . ." (*SP*, 90). His silence and stealth are juxtaposed with Dean's words and actions. There is even a reflection of J. Alfred Prufrock in the narrator when he questions, "Could she, I have often wondered over the empty plates in restaurants, in cafes where only the waiters remain, by any rearrangement of events, by any accident could she, I dream, have become mine? . . . I look in the mirror. Thinning hair. A face marked by lines" (*SP*, 90). His restless yearning mirrors Prufrock's "restless nights" in "sawdust restaurants." Prufrock also worries about the women noticing "how his hair is growing thin," and he wonders about what could have been if he had the courage of his desires.[3] Prufrock backs away from the sexual encounter in deference to stronger, more forceful types just as, in the novel, the narrator allows Dean to preempt what was to be the narrator's own season of rural delight, deferentially admitting "I am only the servant of life. He is an inhabitant" (*SP,* 50). He becomes an observer, one who longs (suffering from *longeur*) for the reality of Anne-Marie and Dean's happiness. His failure to connect serves as Salter's first qualification on "this glorious life": it is not for everyone.

In the shadow of Dean's power, the narrator recedes to spectator, as such a perfect vehicle for telling the story on the practical level and a perfect audience surrogate on the imaginative level. He is a voyeur, and he makes us all voyeurs, trespassing on still another taboo. Stanley Kauffmann proposes that "possibly Salter was trying to build a profane Trinity, a body of Three."[4] Indeed there are a number of triadic relationships in Salter's corpus, the threesome in his story "American Express"; the Irwin Shaw story "Then We Were Three," on which he based his screenplay *Three;* and the chapter in his memoir called "The Captain's Wife," to name only the most prominent. In all these instances, the situation involves two men and a woman they both desire. The dynamic of the threesomes recalls René Girard's description of triangular relationships in the novels of Cervantes, Stendhal, and Proust in his *Deceit, Desire, and the Novel.* Girard explains how the great novelists reveal the imitative nature of desire, how the beloved's desirability in the eyes of the hero is increased by the presence of a mediator's desire for her.[5] In Salter's novel, it was the narrator's interest in this young, attractive but common shop girl that sparked Dean's interest; thereafter, Dean's desire for Anne-Marie increases the narrator's, each man mediating the other's desire. The audience also becomes a party to the triad, identifying with and substituting for one or other of the participants, most commonly perhaps the narrator as we are offered a Peeping-Tom view of the couple's lovemaking. Salter describes the effect: "You are seeing something forbidden, something absolutely natural and unrehearsed; someone unaware of being observed" ("Art," 79).

The narrator also allows us to see ourselves in our various distances from the magical couple, who are as carefree, natural, and acceptable as the elements themselves. By juxtaposing the narrator's yearning with the couple's mutual possession, Salter creates a continuum between yearning and possession with which we may identify depending on our own experiences. Most of us will have to say, like the narrator, "My own life suddenly seems nothing, an old costume, a collection of rags, and I walk, I breathe to the rhythm of his which is stronger than mine" (*SP*, 57). Like the narrator we are left standing in an ordinary, unthrilling, banal world with memories that will not fade.

## Not for Long: The Transient Life

The other qualification the novel makes on "this glorious life" of love and travel is its brevity. Dean's old car, the marvelous Delage, becomes "the very symbol of his existence . . . its dark shape fleeing along the road, that great, spectral car which haunts the villages" (*SP*, 107). There is nothing of permanence about Dean or his time in France with Anne-Marie. As if to remind us, we are constantly made aware of the changing seasons, the story beginning in fall and ending in summer. And in the midst of many scenes of lovemaking, mention is made of the town clock or the passage of time. The narrator says, "I see now that he has always kept himself close to the life that flows, is transient, borne away. And I see his whole appearance differently. He is joined to the brevity of things. He has apprehended at least one great law" (*SP*, 107).

We knew, of course, that Dean and Anne-Marie's time together was enclosed in parentheses rather than being a part of life's text. Dean had never made a commitment, and he could not bear even the thought of introducing Anne-Marie to his father or the circle of their friends. His promises to Anne-Marie were as vague as those of the transient lover, Arthur, in Dreiser's story "The Second Choice." And like Shirley in the same story, Anne-Marie senses that her lover will leave despite his tepid denial: " 'You will go,' she says, 'You are the type' " (*SP*, 59). Their relationship is also shadowed by the specter of Dean's early death. Foreshadowings occur often. The first comes in the Prince of Crayfish story that Anne-Marie invents, in which the Prince, royalty like Dean, ends up in a great frothing kettle (*SP*, 60). And the narrator predicts Dean's end well before the halfway point of the novel when he says "he will be in a poet's grave" before he reaches maturity (*SP*, 76). Later the narrator is even more definitive when talking about the couple as they return home at midnight: "After he was dead I thought often of these moments" (*SP*, 126).

## A Threat to Us All

Because of this last qualification, *A Sport and a Pastime* is more than an interesting experiment in the exotic and the erotic, more than a travel

novel or a love story. More even than a secular sacrament that celebrates
love and travel as one experience. In the way of great literature, it is a
deeply unsettling book. It presents the moments of a clearly ephemeral
relationship—one that the narrator and the reader know will not last—
in such a searing, provocative, and enchanting manner that our whole
belief in the desirability of a normal life, our predisposition toward a
love marked by tranquility and permanence, is challenged.

The utter radiance of a coupling so clearly marked as transient, one
validated only by shared moments, threatens the commitments of love,
marriage, and family that serve as the foundations of our society. If the
threat is only implied during the course of the novel by the ecstatic and
transient nature of the affair, it is made explicit by the book's final paragraph: "As for Anne-Marie, she lives in Troyes now, or did. She is married. I suppose there are children. They walk together on Sundays, the
sunlight falling on them. They visit friends, talk, go home in the
evening, deep in the life we all agree is so greatly to be desired" (*SP*,
180). Margaret Winchell Miller sees the "life we all agree is so greatly to
be desired" as part of the perfection vainly sought in the idyllic affair,
missing the irony of the book's final line. In his *Paris Review* interview
Salter has admitted his intentions were ironic with these last words
("Art," 78). The irony, of course, stems from the contrast between this
imagined future picture of domesticity, this "life we all agree is so
greatly to be desired," and the dazzling display of love, unpredictable
and nomadic, with which we have been drenched. The glory of Dean
and Anne-Marie's impulsive affair, its connection to the life that flows, is
a direct affront to our presumptions of happiness from stability and pre-
dictability.

Dean and Anne-Marie are the choreographers of their own move-
ments. Their improvisations deny responsibility to larger, societal patterns. And their lovemaking flouts all conventions in its obsessiveness.
As Dean slips into bed next to Anne-Marie, the narrator realizes that it
is "an act which threatens us all" (*SP*, 57). Everything about their love is
in sharp contrast to the routines of the life around them. Such domestic
routines are observed and measured by Dean and the narrator in their
dinner with the Jobses, an evening whose "monotony" Dean finds
"incredible," capped by slides of the couple's recent trip to Austria. He
wonders "that there really can be a couple like this" (*SP*, 38), but the
Jobses are the epitome of normalcy. The only other married couple we
get a glimpse of in the novel, Billy and Cristina Wheatland in Paris,
have more glitter and superficial spontaneity, but their routines are any-

thing but unpredictable, with their club-hopping, drinking, and crashing at daybreak.

With Dean and Anne-Marie, on the other hand, every day, every touch is new. Nightly they discover each other. And each encounter is an exploration of desire and a response to desire. Spontaneous movement defines their travel and their love, and as they go from town to town, the great hotels, the very stones sigh approval. In their "atrocities," as the narrator calls them, they become one with France and with the universe. Once in a great old chateau in a small village, Anne-Marie "is able to summon up all of the black countryside that surrounds them, silences in which every object, every form is at rest. The invisible leaves—the night is filled with them—brush one another lightly. The grasses are still" (*SP,* 119). Wherever they go, when Dean "begins to move in and out in long, delirious strokes . . . France is bathed in sunshine. The shops are closed. Churches are filled. In every town, behind locked doors, the restaurants are laying their tables, preparing for lunch" (*SP,* 143). Each variation of love brings them into deeper harmony with their surroundings and undermines our assumption that the regular life "is so greatly to be desired" (*SP,* 180). We are left with a paradox. While the quotidian patterns of couples like the Jobses and the Wheatlands are only in sync with the surface rhythms of life, Dean and Anne-Marie's motions, so irregular and so illicit, make them one with the life around them—the deeper rhythm of seasons, days and nights, and the storied rooms of ancient hotels.

How are we to take this paradox and its implicit challenge to our ordinary lives? We could conceivably dismiss it out of hand on account of the couple's youthfulness. After all, Dean is on holiday like countless American college students and college dropouts, and Anne-Marie is 18. Is not life supposed to be experimental and fraught with adventure in one's green years? Perhaps, but the couple's youth is not the issue, and the narrator, who is older, would change shoes with Dean in a delirious instant if given the chance. If anything, the youthfulness of the couple emphasizes the perpetual challenge that youth issues to maturity. Why does anyone, a boy of 11 asks as he surveys the world of his parents, want to grow up and be an adult? To him adulthood looks like the end of enjoyment. Salter's book, charged with the sexual lightning of youth come of age, echoes this perpetual challenge in language that refuses to fade.

One response to the challenge is shown in *A Son of the Circus* by John Irving's protagonist, Dr. Daruwalla, and his wife, Julia, who on their second honeymoon in Goa discover *A Sport and a Pastime* and read passages aloud as inspiration for their lovemaking. Dr. Daruwalla's delight in Salter's descriptions is surpassed only by his surprise that his wife is equally delighted. The "unexpected stimulation" their marriage receives from the reading is one level of response to the challenge. Irving's fictional interpretation, however, is more sophisticated than seeing Salter's book as bedside stimulation. Daruwalla is, in a sense, Salter's model reader, as he is sensitive to the sting of the book's ending and its parting shot at married life. When Daruwalla feels "the very life he led with Julia—the life he cherished—was being mocked," he questions: "Wasn't there an underlying cruelty to this? Because such a life is 'greatly to be desired,' isn't it? . . . How could anyone expect the married life to compare with the burning intensity of a love affair?"[6] Daruwalla's conclusion, and one presumes Irving's as well, is that Salter is ironic, but not sarcastic in his last line, reading it as less an indictment of marriage than a glorification of sensual love, which is often buried in the baggage of marriage's routines. By breaking out of these routines in their own lovemaking, sparked by the fire of Dean and Anne-Marie, the Daruwallas have indeed made sense of Salter's novel. Daruwalla's reading goes deeper still when he is awakened not just by the novel's sexual charge, but by the creative charge behind its writing. He is overcome by the passion and assurance of Salter's voice, its visionary quality, and this inspires him "to make something up," to find voice for his own inner visions. Daruwalla is Salter's, any author's, ideal reader. He not only interprets the book perceptively, but its passages generate positive changes in his own life. In love and art, he is made new by Salter's story, responding to its core energy. Such a response does not disarm the novel's charge or remove its threat. *A Sport and a Pastime* remains a deeply disturbing book because it endures as a perpetual challenge to the desirability of our own lives.

## Reaction and Assessment

The erotic content of the novel predictably attracted more attention from reviewers than any other aspect, but they did not express the same enthusiasm for it shown by Irving's protagonist. Eliot Fremont-Smith, writing in the *New York Times,* counted 93 specific scenes of sex in fewer than 200 pages, enough to earn the label "sex novel."[7] *The Prairie Schooner* said that Salter catalogs every sexual encounter of the couple "in such lingering detail that it verges on the pornographic" ("Bookmarks,"

448). And the *Library Journal* discouraged library purchase on the basis of the "vigorous 'love' scenes," narrated "in language suitable for telling it to the marines."[8] Stanley Kauffmann, more benignly, labeled the novel's view of sex "romantic" and found it "a frequently touching attempt to remake the universe in terms of a passion at its fullest" (Kauffman, 24).

The two most influential reviews, in *Time* and the *New York Times Book Review,* were positive. The former felt "this curiously distilled method of storytelling proves effective and makes something lyrical of a rather commonplace romance."[9] And Webster Schott, writing in the latter, called the book "a tour de force in erotic realism, a romantic cliffhanger, an opaline vision of Americans in France."[10] However, even the reviewers who liked the book, such as Kauffmann and Schott, categorized it as "minor." And *Time* concluded with a sentence that seemed to recognize that the audience for the novel would remain small: "There are bestselling novelists who could learn from this cool and quiet book" (*Time,* 122). Over the years, especially since the novel was reissued in a North Point edition in 1985, critical enthusiasm has grown. Anatole Broyard, an influential critic, called the novel's style "brilliant" in a review of a later Salter book.[11] *The Washington Post* wrote: "In lists of neglected classics one of the most frequently mentioned is Salter's hauntingly beautiful novel," whose "spirit—the ache and artistry of Scott Fitzgerald filtered though the cool sensibility of Flaubert or James—evokes France, missed opportunities, all the fugitive beauty of youth."[12] Reynolds Price's previously quoted canonization of the novel was offered in response to a *New York Times Book Review*'s query regarding favorite opening paragraphs in 1985. Novelist Elizabeth Benedict, in a 1985 review, thought the novel "remarkable" and Salter's prose "as careful and light as a structure made of eggshells."[13]

With its status as an underground classic now confirmed by the Modern Library's distinguished editorial board, *A Sport and a Pastime* seems destined to be a book for the ages. Justifiably. The novel has a haunting quality, largely because of its language and its peculiar emotional positioning of the narrator in relation to the two main characters and their feast. From the start the narrator's tone is nostalgic, as if he is returning all over in the telling to that year in Autun, or was it Auxerre, or perhaps Chaumont, where Salter lived in 1961. The idea of a return to the past is reinforced when he says at the end of the first chapter, "I am thirty; I am thirty-four—the years turn dry as leaves" (*SP,* 9). In other words, he was 30 when the events took place; he is now 34 in the telling, giving his tale the weight of time gone by. Like Nick Carraway, the narrator must return in order to bring light and perspective to the hero's deeds, which in turn illuminate our own desires.

I picture the narrator sitting down at a desk with his photographs of the town and the couple scattered before him. "These are notes," he writes, "to photographs of Autun. It would be better to say they began as notes but became something else, a description of what I conceive to be events" (*SP*, 10–11). He begins his love song, again like Prufrock, without fear of self-disclosure, fearlessly offering himself to be our guide through his recollections. "They were meant for me alone, but I no longer hide them. Those times are past" (*SP*, 11). He shows us not only provincial France, but the role of love in visiting it or any foreign land. He is sure in his recollections because of his own desire, creating Dean when necessary, but little fabrication is needed, for he has become one with Dean in his love for Anne-Marie Costallat and for France. Writing about Proust's *The Past Recaptured,* René Girard says, "It is the transcendent quality of a former desire which is relived on contact with a relic of the past." The relic, Girard explains, has "all of the virtues of a sacrament" (Girard, 80). This perfectly describes the narrator's position and tone in reference to the events he reverently relives. His photographs are his relics, his pictures of Dean and Anne-Marie and of "Autun, still as a churchyard. Tile roofs, dark with moss. The amphitheatre. The great, central square: the Champ de Mars. Now, in the blue of autumn, it reappears, this old town, provincial autumn that touches the bone" (*SP*, 9). The hushed, measured rhythms of Salter's style initiate the reader into the sacramental nature of this pilgrimage of love. The novel itself becomes the ultimate relic of "the transcendent quality of a former desire," Anne-Marie's, Dean's, the narrator's, Salter's, and now ours.

## Chapter Five
# From Song to Sonata *(Light Years)*

Eight years elapsed between the publication of *A Sport and a Pastime* and Salter's next novel, *Light Years* (1975). During the interval, he continued his career as screenwriter and journalist, forging a lasting friendship with producer and editor Robert Emmett Ginna, who engaged Salter to do a film script about an Eastern European dictatorship. The undertaking involved initial transatlantic flights for research and, once the writing was done, later trips to persuade actors and directors to commit to the project. The resultant script had a shadow history of more than six years in which various actors and directors—names like Joseph Losey, Paul Scofield, Vanessa Redgrave, Max Schell—drifted in and out of the picture. The critical piece never fell into place, and the film was not made. As Salter ruefully admits, "[T]he hardest fought campaigns may not end in victory" (*BD,* 282). At this time Salter also was busy writing short stories, publishing his first in the *Paris Review* in 1968. Editor George Plimpton was among the early discoverers of Salter's talent, and he took three more stories in short order, which appeared in the *Paris Review* between 1970 and 1972.

Some of the concerns of these early stories, most noticeably the precariousness of relationships and the perils of artistic ambitions, reappear in *Light Years,* which was written between 1972 and 1973 in Aspen, Colorado. Salter had first visited Aspen in 1959, and in 1962 he purchased a house there for $12,000, using it as a summer residence during the years 1962 to 1967. In 1969 he settled in Aspen, making it his year-round residence until 1980, when he began shuttling back and forth between there and Long Island (summers), a pattern he continues to this day. So it was in Aspen that Salter wrote his novel about a family living near the Hudson River within commuting distance of New York City, just as he had written about provincial France while in a Manhattan apartment. Why do writers so often write about one place while living in another? Ibsen wrote of Norway while in Denmark and Italy, Joyce of Dublin while in France, Hemingway of Northern Michigan while in Paris. Distance seems to sharpen both perspective and desire. Certainly in Salter's case remoteness from his settings induced a nostalgia that became part of the spirit of the books. He allowed to me that "being removed may occasion some longing to write about a place" (PI, Guggenheim). And about the genesis of *Light Years,* he has acknowledged: "I had in mind a casting back, a final rich confession, as it were. There was a line of Jean Renoir's that struck me: The only things that are important in life are those you remember. That was to be the key. It was to be a book of pure recall" (*BD,* 331).

## The Personal Connection

*Light Years* is imbued from its opening lines with a nostalgic tone: "We dash the black river, its flats smooth as stone. Not a ship, not a dinghy, not one cry of white. The water lies broken, cracked from the wind. This great estuary is wide, endless. . . . We flash the wide river, a dream of the past. . . . And on wings like the gulls, soar up, turn, look back" (*LY,* 3). Clearly Salter was looking back at what his own life had been like in New City, New York, in this novel about a couple with a taste for the finer things, who are raising two daughters in the idyllic exurbs of New York City. The tone and subject matter of the novel are directly traceable to Salter's intense memories from the 1960s. On a purely pictorial level—as a sunlit evocation of family life in a setting at once pastoral and urbane—the book is a masterpiece. Birthdays, bedtime routines, games with the children, meals, trips to the city, holidays, dinners with friends—all glow in the burnished perfection of memory's fond stroking. Whole seasons are summoned in an instant: "Summer. The foliage is thick. The leaves shimmer everywhere like scales. In the morning, aroma of coffee, the whiteness of sunlight across the floor. The sound of Franca upstairs, of a young girl's steps as she made her bed, combed her hair, descended with the warm smile of youth" (*LY,* 111).

Salter drew on the capital of his own life to fund much of the book's emotional commitment to a certain way of living. His paternal feelings, attachment to a refined lifestyle, and artistic aspirations provided a bank of experience to secure the novel's affective risks. His own children, then four in number, ranged in age from 10 to 17 when he began writing *Light Years,* engendering the novel's touching refrain of parental concern in sentiments such as this: "He [Viri] longs for the one line to give them [his children] that they will always remember, that will embrace everything, that will point the way, but he cannot find the line, he cannot recognize it" (*LY,* 45). The delightful interplay between Viri and his two daughters recalls the playful exchanges between Charlie Waters and his daughter,

Honoria, in Fitzgerald's "Babylon Revisited." As well, Salter's fondness
for beautiful surroundings and for good food and wine animate the living patterns of Viri and Nedra Berland. "Life," he writes, "is meals.
Lunches on a blue checkered cloth on which salt has spilled. The smell
of tobacco. Brie, yellow apples, wood-handled knives" (*LY,* 25). Salter's
own style of living asserts the essential connection between the daily
pleasures of food, drink, and surroundings and the eternal pleasure of
art, and this connection informs the lifestyle of the Berlands.

When Salter made Viri an architect with aspirations for fame and a
reverence for exemplars, the author drew upon his own artistic attitudes.
The following paragraph about Viri Berland is pure Salter, a formulation
of his own credo: "He believed in greatness. He believed in it as if it
were a virtue, as if it could be his own. . . . He was clear-eyed and exact
about the value of other people's work. Toward his own he maintained a
mild respect. In his faith, at the heart of his illusions, was the structure
that would appear in photographs of his time, the famous building he
had created and that nothing—no criticism, no envy, not even demolition—could alter" (*LY,* 34). Salter would probably admit, in a manner
both modest and ambitious, that at the heart of his own illusions, both
then and now, is the faith that *Light Years* and *A Sport and a Pastime* are
structures worthy to "appear in photographs of his time," resistant to
criticism, envy, and demolition. He confesses that when he first read his
editor's final blue-penciled comment on the manuscript of *Light Years,*
"an absolutely marvelous book in every way," his hopes soared. "I
wanted praise, of course, widespread praise . . . I wanted glory" (*BD,*
332). And even years later, he says about the book in his understated
manner that it "still doesn't displease. I find it satisfying" ("Art," 81).

While he was writing *Light Years,* which shows the disintegration of a
marriage, Salter's own was coming apart. He and his wife, Ann, were
divorced in 1975, the same year the book was published. Undoubtedly
his own experience contributed to his understanding of how such a
neatly wrapped package, which included adored children, could come
undone. He acknowledges in his memoir that the original impulse
behind the book was "to summarize certain attitudes towards life,
among them that marriage lasted too long. I was perhaps thinking of
my own" (*BD,* 331). Salter, nevertheless, insists that the couple in the
book are not he and his wife. When questioned directly, he says, "The
book was not about my marriage. Really. It was modeled on a couple
who didn't get a divorce until four or five years afterwards, but I could
see it coming; others could too" (PI, Algonquin). This explanation is the

same he gave me about the book's origin when I first interviewed him in 1985. It rings true, for in further questioning Salter about his own divorce, I got the impression that, among other differences, it was anything but the amicable and mutually supportive parting that is pictured in the novel.

## Structure

Like *A Sport and a Pastime,* which is a song of love and travel, *Light Years* also has the lilt of a musical composition. With its five-part structure and greater heft, however, it is more sonata than song, each part a movement repeating the earlier themes of the charm of family life, the weight of marriage, the care for children, the search for glory, the process of aging, and the beauty of moments. The flow is chronological, beginning when the couple are in their late twenties and following them to their late forties, but the events are not exhaustively continuous or without lapses.

The first movement begins in 1958 with Nedra and Viri Berland and their two daughters, seven and five, living what might be called, after the book Nedra reads, Earthly Paradise. We glimpse the comfortable routines of Nedra and Viri's life together and the joys of their separate love affairs. Part 2 begins in 1963, showing the family at Christmas, Easter, on summer vacation in Amagansett, and Viri and Nedra socializing with friends. Viri is rejected by his lover, Kaya, and Nedra's father dies. In part 3, which opens in 1967, we see Nedra casting aside her lover, Jivan, and taking a new one, Andre Orlosky, a poet she meets at Jivan's. The girls are coming of age. A close friend of the family, Arnaud, is beaten and loses an eye. Nedra finally convinces Viri to take her to Europe, and at the end of the trip, in 1970, she tells him their life must change. Part 4 begins with them living in the house together until their divorce is granted in November. In the aftermath, on his own, Viri reels in self-pity and confusion; Nedra goes to Europe, lives for a while with a lover, returns to the States, and fails in her audition with a theatrical company but not with the company's leading man. Franca begins work in the publishing field, and the men are all smitten. Danny, the Berlands' younger daughter, marries. Peter Daro, a good friend, dies of a mysterious illness. The final movement finds Viri selling the house and going to Italy, where at 47, he is revived by the love of a younger Italian woman, who becomes his emotionally dependent wife. Nedra becomes ill and, after a visit from Franca in her cabin by the sea, dies suddenly.

The book ends with Viri returning alone to their former dwelling along the river's shore.

Each of the larger parts is divided into short sections that feature scenes from the Berlands' life, sometimes following one another closely in time, sometimes involving considerable intervals. Scenes frequently jump from season to season or from birthday to holiday, Salter carefully marking the temporal progression so important to his theme. He selects sparingly the occasions that give shape and substance to the days and hours of Viri and Nedra's marriage. Casual moments become friezes that define the world they have created and reveal the seemingly insignificant impulses and gestures that will determine its future.

As a screenwriter Salter had become familiar with such cinematic techniques as jump cuts, telescopic narrowing or enlargement, and montage, and it shows in the novel. At times he will switch abruptly from one scene to another as when Viri is alone in his lover Kaya's apartment, crazily cutting the heart out of her best dress in his hurt and anger over discovering her with another man, still daydreaming about her nakedness, and the scene changes suddenly to: "Nedra was happy that evening. She seemed pleased with herself" (*LY,* 85). The effect is jarring, showing how much drama lies below the surface of their marriage.

Similarly, in a brilliant use of montage, paragraphs describing a dinner scene with Jivan as the Berlands' guest alternate with paragraphs describing Jivan and Nedra in bed in his apartment. The two scenes resonate in subtle and revealing ways: Jivan lights a fire in the family hearth, and Nedra leaves his apartment "like a stone warmed for bed in the evening" (*LY,* 64); the dinner is at dusk, the lovemaking at noon; Jivan dresses carefully for the dinner in an ascot and white shirt and responds attentively to Viri's remarks, while the lovers are naked and silent. By juxtaposing the two scenes, Salter seems to imply that our lives are easily compartmentalized and a love affair need not overtly infringe on a marriage. The Berlands' oldest daughter, Franca, however, senses the charge between her mother and Jivan, indicating that the energies cannot be so neatly packaged. She is also alert to the attentions of Jivan, and we sense she will soon become a woman like her mother. The more lasting impression of the chapter is an appreciation for the contrasting pleasures of domestic contentment and infidelity, both alluring, especially when one's lover is also a family friend. Salter is never better than when showing the rhythms of life, and the accomplishment of this chapter is its simultaneous portrait of the rhythms of two opposite ways of life, neither as easily contained as it at first appears.

## The Heart of the Novel

*Light Years* can be read as a sequel to *A Sport and a Pastime,* not in the usual sense of a continuing cast of characters, but in that Viri and Nedra Berland are well along the worn path of conjugal life that Anne-Marie Costallat is just entering at the conclusion of the earlier book. The Berlands—living with their two daughters on the west bank of the Hudson River in a graced circle of comfort, beauty, kindness, and culture—enact a delightful variation of domestic life, "the life we all agree is so greatly to be desired," more desirable surely than Anne-Marie was ever likely to find. And Salter explores this life unflinchingly, frankly confronting its desirability as he traces the irony of its subtle unwinding.

The novel memorializes the beauty of a marriage in the process of disintegration, and Salter is unfailingly sympathetic toward the couple and their creation "of conjugal life in its purest, most generous form" (*LY,* 197). There are no villains but the villainies of routine and boredom, eventually found to be inextricable from marriage itself, and the overriding villainy of time, whose unseen might destroys all, but for the defiant monuments of memory.

The cover of the 1985 North Point edition of *Light Years* features an impressionist painting, "The Breakfast Room," by Pierre Bonnard. The scene is a table, covered with a white tablecloth, with breakfast dishes and food, all framed in the background by a glass door looking out over a second-story porch and onto the brown-flecked greenery of large oaks. The painting captures the atmosphere of the novel and typifies the relative uneventfulness of its movement, small, commonplace acts that mount eventually into cumulative significance. "There is no complete life. There are only fragments. We are born to have nothing, to have it pour through our hands. And yet, this pouring, this flood of encounters, struggles, dreams . . . one must be unthinking, like a tortoise. One must be resolute, blind" (*LY,* 35–36). *Light Years* is about the passage of time, both the eternity of moments and the way these have of slipping by, not only into the past but even into forgetfulness.

### The Course of a Marriage

The lives of Nedra and Viri Berland have burgeoned into the ripeness of late summer. We see the fineness of the fabric they have woven: the beauty of their home, the loveliness of their two daughters, the delicate understanding behind their own relationship, and their relaxed community with friends who are constantly visiting or being visited. Viri, an architect, yearns for fame. He is "sensitive to lives that had, beneath their surface, like a huge rock or shadow, a glory that would be discovered, that would rise one day to the light" (*LY,* 34). Nedra, at the age of 28, possesses a beauty enormously influential on those around her; she is tall, luminous, "a woman with long legs, a graceful neck, on her forehead the faintest creases of the decade to come" (*LY,* 26). Nedra, however, is ambivalent about her body, for while she at times "felt its immortality," she knows it "would one day betray her" (*LY,* 115).

Nedra's superior grasp of reality and her greater capacity for action make her the novel's strongest character and the most fully developed female in Salter's fiction. Although the couple both have affairs, Nedra knows long before Viri that their marriage is dead, incapable of nourishing their deepest longings. She had already shown her strength by ending her affair with Jivan and beginning another with a man she met at Jivan's apartment. Nedra acts, while Viri drifts in a daze after he is jilted by his lover, Kaya. During the couple's trip to Europe, Nedra confirms how thoroughly her life has revolved around Viri and the girls and their home, and she determines that this must change. Europe, its depth and variety, intensifies her awareness of the unlived life, just as it had for any number of Henry James's protagonists. "I don't want to go back to our old life," she casually tells Viri over dinner in a restaurant outside London (*LY,* 200). After their divorce she returns to Europe to find a degree of happiness in her solitude, her confidence, and in the effect she has on men: "She was an elegant being again, alone, admired. . . . It was the opening of the triumph to which her bare room in the Bellevue entitled her, as a schoolroom entitles one to dazzling encounters, to nights of love" (*LY,* 213).

## Time's Power

Time is the principal antagonist in the novel. Its effect on the characters' lives is largely destructive, for it swallows up the sunlight days, seals the smallest decisions with the stamp of finality and irreversibility, and blurs even memory itself. And yet, in the face of time's overwhelming power, Salter asserts there are moments that will never be erased, moments that are preserved in the mind and made eternal by the monument of style.

Nedra's triumph is rushed by the flow of time. After her father's death she sensed there was no longer a buffer zone between herself and death: "It was finished, done. Suddenly she felt it all through her like an omen. She was exposed. The way was clear for her own end" (*LY,* 149). Alone now at 41, she struggles to preserve the remnants of her once electrifying beauty:

> She stepped back. How to re-create that tall young woman whose laugh turned people's heads, whose dazzling smile fell on gatherings like money on restaurant tables, snow on country houses, morning at sea? She took up her implements, eye pencil, cucumber cream, lipstick the color of isinglass. . . . Finally she was satisfied. In a certain light, with the right background, the right clothes, a beautiful coat . . . yes, and she had her smile, it was all that was left from the early days, it was hers, she would have it always, the way one always remembers how to swim. (*LY,* 208)

Women in the novel, as perhaps in life, suffer most poignantly the manifestations of the passing years and their consequences. Because of her age, 43, Nedra fails in her acting audition before the great director and teacher Philip Kasine. She and her friend Eve and other women in the novel frequently are caught observing the changes in their bodies and revealing their most intimate fears of physical dissolution. Her friend Nora asks Nedra, "Do we really only have one season? One summer . . . and it's over?" (*LY,* 140). With Salter's pictures of Nedra's daughters awakening into their bodies as adolescents, then taking full possession of them as dazzling beauties in their twenties, the novel portrays the seven ages of women, including the stage at which Nedra transfers her deepest longings vicariously to her daughters. Even old age is included in a brief exchange between Viri's second wife, Lia, and her 80-year-old housekeeper, whose fears of death are calmed by Lia's empty reassurances. And Nedra at 47 runs swiftly past the last stages in her sudden illness and end.

Both sexes, of course, march to time's egalitarian cadence. Death lurks in the background for men and women alike, sometimes breaking into the circle of their consciousness, as when a close friend of the Berlands, Peter Daro, contracts a rare disease and quickly dies, or earlier when the family hear of the death of the little girl who had already lost a leg to cancer. In the end, death claims Nedra herself. And symbolically Viri, too, for he, who has thus far spent most of his time avoiding the unpleasant things Nedra had always faced head-on (such as the problems of their marriage), at the end of the novel calmly contemplates his own end. Viri has entered into a marriage more deadening than his first. One of their daughters, Danny, is married and has a lover, her husband's brother, and two children; Franca likely will marry and follow suit.

Probably they will construct lives more similar to, than different from, their parents'. Time flows on.

Another of *Light Years*'s insights into time is the cumulative effect of our smallest actions. "For whatever we do," Salter writes, "even whatever we do not do prevents us from doing the opposite. Acts demolish their alternatives, that is the paradox. So that life is a matter of choices, each one final and of little consequence, like dropping stones into the sea" (*LY,* 36). The pattern of Viri and Nedra's daily life, not simply their dramatic acts of unfaithfulness, leads to their ultimate fates. The novel presents the affairs themselves as the result of other smaller, discrete actions, the accumulation of which becomes a kind of boredom. Given their individual capacities for passion, ambition, and adventure, and the ultimate lack of room within the narrow road of conjugal life for these to be exercised, their affairs are natural outgrowths. Their life together shifts as surely as the banks of a river are altered by an underwater current. The novel's tone eschews the operatic. It portrays the believable burden of the mundane, the terrible consequences of the feelings we have over our bread and cheese in the morning and our gin and tonics at night. In this regard, the tone and method are reminiscent of Flaubert and Joyce's *Dubliners.*

Ultimately the novel shows us time not only cutting down the endless days that our youthful imagination projects for us but even destroying our memories of the past, the most devastating affront. The years are light years because of their beauty, yes, but also because of their fragility, their rapidity, their evanescence. Nedra poignantly illustrates this as she tells Eve of her inability to remember the face of her early lover, who at 40 brought her, a girl of 17, to the city of New York for the first time. This blurring of the past is part of the unavoidable toll of time that is the focus of the novel. "The present is powerful. Memories fade" (*LY,* 303).

## The Monument of Language

Against this blurring, however, stands the indelible quality of certain moments. After the family have spent a lovely summer at Amagansett, Salter writes: "They did not know what they were praising; the days, the sense of contentment, the pagan joy. They were acclaiming the summer of their lives in which, far from danger, they rested. Their flesh was speaking, their well-being" (*LY,* 113–14). One comes away from *Light Years* with an appreciation for the radiance as well as the transience of these moments of glory, an appreciation that derives largely from the author's style, which is marvelous, spare, and totally fresh. Reviewers and critics call Salter's style "impressionistic" (Miller, 3). I would, in fact, press the analogy to painting even more. The impressionist painters employ vivid color to capture the beauty of mundane life. Their unrealistic hues and selective brush strokes permit the viewer to see familiar objects in a new way. Like the magician, impressionists rely on the viewer's willing collaboration in the illusion of reality presented. Salter uses such a technique. He creates a magical effect out of selected detail, cadence, and sound, conjuring up both the illusion of reality and its ultimately inexpressible beauty. Salter knows that his magic relies on the reader's familiarity with the experience itself, which can never be captured, any more than the magic of human vision can be captured by the artist. It can only be evoked.

Emerson said that the poet differs from the masses only in the ability to put into words what others experience. The poet must write from personal experience and must say it truthfully, and all will know that it is so. Beneath this theory lies the assumption that out of the particularity of private experience the poet's words call forth the assent of common experience. This particularity need not be an exhaustive one, only such as is required to appeal to the inner experience of each reader. Salter plays an impressionist variation on Emerson's concept. His style uses bits and pieces of reality, like an artist using pigments and dots, to create an illusion of reality. "The days had lost their warmth. Sometimes at noon, as if in farewell, there was an hour or two like summer, swiftly gone. On the stands in nearby orchards were hard, yellow apples filled with powerful juice. They exploded against the teeth, they spat white flecks like arguments. In the distant fields, seas of dank earth far from towns, there were still tomatoes clinging to the vines. At first glance it seemed only a few, but they were hidden, sheltered; that was how they had survived" (*LY*, 73). If we look too closely, we can see the individual brush strokes and the lack of elaborate detail. If we step back, however, we know that this is life, and we fill in the missing details as surely as our eye reconstructs the impressionist painting into a fully recognizable scene.

Richard Poirier asserts that "the classic American writers try through style temporarily to free the hero (and the reader) from systems, to free them from the pressures of time, biology, economics, and from the social forces which are ultimately the undoing of American heroes and quite often of their creators."[1] Salter writes in this manner. In *Light Years,* he

tries through style to free his characters from the press of time and the
social forces behind the institution of marriage. At the end, although
they seem to have partially transcended the latter, Nedra and Viri are
both crushed by time. What remains, however, are the sentences that
describe their joys and "play a constant sacrament of praise" for all who
hear. Of the couple's two granddaughters, Salter writes:

> Perhaps they would read aloud as Viri had done on those long winter
> evenings, those idle summers when, in a house by the sea, it seemed the
> family he had created would always endure. Certainly they would be pas-
> sionate and tall and one day give to their children—there is no assurance
> of this, we imagine it, we cannot do otherwise—marvelous birthdays,
> huge candle-rich cakes, contests, guessing games, not many young
> guests, six or eight, a room that leads to a garden, from afar one can hear
> the laughing, the doors open suddenly, out they run into the long, sweet
> afternoon. (*LY,* 303 – 4)

In such sentences, strewn about the novel like strains from Peter
Quince's clavier or scenes painted on a Grecian urn (Keats is mentioned), Salter preserves the memories of moments that could not last.
The novel itself becomes the ultimate monument to the fleeting hours
and days, not in its story, which tracks the inevitable ravages of time,
but in its style, which preserves the shining remnants.

"Every style," says Susan Sontag, "is a means of insisting on something."[2] Salter's style, like any author's, insists on different things at different times. But one of its constant characteristics is simplicity, insisting
on the elemental things of life: light, morning, evening, ambition, food,
drink, desire, shared moments. It attends to such things with extraordinary precision and absolute devotion, ultimately carving a memorial in
words that resists the pressures that will ultimately defeat his protagonists.

Near the novel's end Salter uses two symbols of continuity to suggest
that such memorials will always survive. The first occurs when Franca
visits her dying mother and is told for the first time the stories her
grandfather used to tell Nedra as a child. Overcome by the bond of
emotion these and other stories about her grandfather and her father
bring her, Franca takes Nedra's hand and kisses it. Language has transcended death, the death of Nedra's father, Nedra's own death, and it
now lives on in her daughter. The second symbol occurs when Viri
returns to the grounds of their old house by the river and discovers the
tortoise on whose shell the family had scratched their initials long ago

when all was green and golden. "He stopped in disbelief. How it had escaped the cars, the keen eyes of children, of dogs, he could not understand, but somehow it had" (*LY,* 307). Like a book, the tortoise had survived the perils of the years, and on its shell (cover) stood their initials, emblems of language, recalling a time gone by. Although the tortoise "acknowledged nothing," Viri is changed, for he senses in the reptile's existence the continued life of the times they had. "It seemed the woods [words] were breathing, that they had recognized him, made him their own. He sensed the change. He was moved as if deeply grateful. The blood sprang within him, rushed from his head" (*LY,* 308). As with the classic American writers who were his forebears, Salter succeeds through his style in defying the forces, particularly that of time, that defeat his characters.

Another thing that Salter's style insists on, which further attaches him to the American tradition, is the power of language itself. Nedra reads a book on Kandinsky: "The book was in her lap; she had read no further. The power to change one's life comes from a paragraph, a lone remark. The lines that penetrate us are slender, like the flukes that live in river water and enter the bodies of swimmers. She was excited, filled with strength. The polished sentences had arrived, it seemed, like so many other things, at just the right time. How can we imagine what our lives should be without the illumination of the lives of others?" (*LY,* 161). This short paragraph describes the ability of language to change lives. What Nedra had just read is that when Kandinsky went back to Russia at the beginning of the first war, "he left behind the woman—she was a painter, too—that he'd been living with for ten years. He saw her again just once—imagine this—at an exhibition in 1927" (*LY,* 161). And this remark is the catalyst for Nedra to leave Viri.

Salter's own lines constantly strive for such illuminations, and his success is illustrated in many of the preceding quotations, often the effect of a final sentence of a paragraph that crystallizes what has gone before. Another example is a brief paragraph that captures the attraction of family life: "There is no happiness like this happiness: quiet mornings, light from the river, the weekend ahead. They lived a Russian life, a rich life, interwoven, in which the misfortune of one, a failure, illness, would stagger them all. It was like a garment, this life. Its beauty was outside, its warmth within" (*LY,* 69). The final sentence is typical Salter, in which a found metaphor, the garment of their life, is suddenly shown to have more dimensions, a deeper revelation than was at first thought. This revelation is delivered in a short dagger of a sentence.

One could easily imagine a reader of the novel having her life changed by such lines in exactly the opposite way that Nedra is changed by the lines from the biography of Kandinsky.
Numerous literary references within the novel, most of them to dramatic works, attest to Salter's respect for the power of literature to change lives. Viri plays a performance of Kipling's *The Elephant's Child* for his children; Franca at 12 writes a story, "The Queen of Feathers"; at a dinner party the guest of honor is writing a biography about the children of famous writers and artists; Nedra goes to Davos, scene of *The Magic Mountain;* when Viri attends a revival of Ibsen's *The Master Builder*, it hits him like an accusation of his own artistic mediocrity; Brom, Nedra's actor-lover, offers as explanation of his disbelief in marriage *The Bhagavad-Gita;* Peter Daro suggests the example of Nora Helmer in *A Doll's House* as explanation of Nedra's kind of happiness; and a couple's reaction to *The Cherry Orchard* is described by Daro. Finally, as a parallel to Nedra's change coming about through the biography of Kandinsky, Viri is reading a biography of Montaigne when he, like Montaigne, falls in love with an Italian woman during a journey there. Once more life imitates art.

## Reaction and Assessment

Although I have not seen the charge leveled at this particular novel of Salter, I could well imagine a criticism of it as lacking a moral center. It is true that Salter is easy on his protagonists, laying no blame for the divorce. Nedra is clearly the instigator, and it is she who brings down the final curtain. An earlier character, Catherine Daro, had commented that Nedra was the most selfish creature on earth. Yet Salter balances her selfishness in the novel against Viri's torpor, his willingness to list with the tides and not confront hard truths. Salter understands these traits and presents them as part of the larger picture of Viri's and Nedra's personalities. He is clear-eyed about the problems within the marriage but dewy-eyed about its splendid moments. When the divorce is finally accomplished, he comments as omniscient narrator, "I wish it could have been otherwise" (*LY,* 203). In entering so thoroughly and nonjudgmentally into the lives of the Berlands, Salter has performed the ultimate moral act of the novelist, understanding. He has also shown how irrelevant is blame when the causes of an action like divorce reside in the cumulative patterns of our lives and when the results of the action are so ambiguous.

Two influential reviewers attacked *Light Years,* particularly its style, rather savagely. Anatole Broyard thought that Salter's language, which he had described as brilliant in *A Sport and a Pastime,* showed signs of degeneration, though the review does not make clear what he meant by this. He gives three examples, one without explanation, one with an explanation that has nothing to do with style, and the third with a derisive dismissal. In the last example, when Nedra, still lonely in a German hotel room after leaving Viri, thinks, "[S]wallows were screaming over the stained roofs of Rome," Broyard spoofs, "Why Rome? Because it's baroque, dummy!" (Broyard, 41). The reviewer's question, of course, is facetious and his comment disingenuous, because one sentence later Salter had written in explanation: "She was pulled by terrestrial forces to places far away. She could not seem to summon herself into the present, into an hour as empty as that before a storm" (*LY,* 207–8). We had also just been told at the beginning of the chapter that Nedra feared she had made a mistake in choosing Davos in winter because of its oppressiveness. Are thoughts of Rome, then, so baroque? I suspect Broyard's underlying feelings have little to do with style, for he says Salter's "prose is still rich and ambitious, but it seems exiled in the house on the Hudson where the characters live" (Broyard, 41). In referring to the couple's "alleged incompatibility" (which, by the way, is incorrect; they are wonderfully compatible) and in making fun of Nedra's quest ("It is not enough to be content . . . . We must cut every tie"), Broyard seems personally affronted by the novel's drift toward the dissolution of the Berlands' marriage. Did it strike a nerve?

Robert Towers's review in the *New York Times Book Review* began innocently enough with feigned praise such as: " 'Light Years' is a very classy book," and "the book provides a feast for lovers of 'fine' writing," but the quotation marks around the "fine" should have been a clue to Towers's real feelings about Salter's "relentlessly poetic prose, an unearned lyricism that envelops the novel like Muzak."[3] As example, Towers quotes the following: "The air overhead, glittering, infinite, the moist earth beneath—one could taste this earth, its richness, its density, bathe in the air like a stream." Even when they are quoted out of context, it's hard to know what makes such lyrical sentences "unearned" in Towers's eyes. Of course, when the sentence is seen within its paragraph, it length and lyricism contrast quite nicely with the brevity and factuality of the surrounding sentences. Here is the sentence in context: "In the morning the light came in silence. The house slept. The air overhead, glittering, infinite, the moist earth beneath—one could taste this earth, its rich-

ness, its density, bathe in the air like a stream. Not a sound. The rind of
the cheese had dried like bread. The glasses held the stale aroma of van-
ished wine" (*LY,* 67). Reviewers, of course, are limited in space, but they
should not be limited in fairness. Yet Towers's only remark about the
offending sentence is "On and on," as if Salter had no sense of timing
and had strung together such poetic flights with no regard for the
grainy particulars of the text, which is simply untrue. Towers must have
had some doubts about his criticism, for he admits, "In fairness it must
be said that, as one reads on, the strained lyricism becomes less intru-
sive." Whatever doubts existed, however, are quickly dismissed in the
guillotine of his final remark: "An overwritten, chi-chi, and rather silly
novel" (Towers, 7).

Overall, reviewer reactions ran the gamut. Elizabeth Benedict
described it as "a masterpiece about the life of a family" and an
"immensely moving book."[4] Lee Grove praised it as "a really great"
American novel, only one of three in five years to make her "tremble so
violently" that she had to run outside after finishing it.[5] Some reviewers
did not care for Salter's protagonists. Ronald De Feo found them "simply not interesting or complex enough";[6] and John Mellors felt they
were "too precious to be true."[7] On the other hand, Benedict said, "One
falls in love with this family" (Benedict 1986, 143); Barbara A. Bannon
judged that "all the characters are skillfully created in a special book";[8]
and James Wolcott praised Salter for avoiding "a narcissistic exercise"
and creating "an unexpectedly moving ode to beautiful lives frayed by
time."[9]

Only a couple of reviews devoted any space to interpretation. Dun-
can Fallowell archly asserted, "The book is about food and drink" and
proceeded to gorge his review with some of Salter's many references to
this subject.[10] One assumes that Fallowell's clever review was strictly
tongue in cheek, for saying that *Light Years* is about food and drink is
rather like saying Joyce's "The Dead" is about a dinner party. On
another level entirely from all the other reviews was Sven Birkerts's.
Birkerts saw the novel as a tragedy of character—"explicitly moody,
tender, elegiac"—in the sense that "tragedy is fate," and "in spite of the
love and companionship [Viri and Nedra] share, their energies are fun-
damentally alien."[11] So the book is about "the breaking of invisible
human threads. . . . The process is slow, painful and reluctantly under-
gone. Each broken filament is a consequence of forces and needs that are
felt but in no way understood. Impulse, longing, change—these are
mysterious and irreducible. And in this respect one does not feel that

Viri and Nedra have betrayed each other. If anything has betrayed them it is time itself, time rearing up against the heedless optimism of a present that cannot believe that things will change" (Birkerts, 757). Birkerts's comment on Salter's method of elision in structuring of the novel is also incisive: "What finally emerges is a narrative that corresponds to life as it is felt and remembered; the elisions are the same kind that we practice on our own experience" (Birkerts, 757). Birkerts reads perceptively and writes gracefully, illustrating by his brief but penetrating critique the difference between understanding and reaction in reviewing.

Reviewers noticed the prevalence of images of light throughout the novel, but no one mentioned the equally important image of the river. One of the novel's tentative titles had been *Estuarial Lives* before Salter settled on *Light Years*. The Berlands' home is set high on the banks of the Hudson, and the river is associated with the comfort and scope of their lifestyle as well as all the daily joys that constitute the fabric of domestic bliss. Salter begins the novel with the river, explicitly associating it with the passage of time. "We flash the wide river, a dream of the past" (*LY*, 3). The path of the marriage itself, like that of some rivers, divides into two streams, allowing Viri and Nedra to go their separate ways, inexorably driven by their personal currents but losing the force and majesty of their combined energies. And the book ends where it began, on the banks of the river, literally still the Hudson, but metaphorically the river of time, the river whose course changes inevitably and imperceptibly, the river fed by smaller streams, the river rushing all too rapidly to the sea: "He [Viri] reaches the water's edge. There is the dock, unused now, with its flaking paint and rotten boards, its underpilings drenched in green. Here at the great, dark river, here on the bank. It happens in an instant. It is all one long day, one endless afternoon, friends leave, we stand on the shore. Yes, he thought, I am ready, I have always been ready, I am ready at last" (*LY*, 308). The contradiction between the last two statements mirrors the contradiction of life itself, lived always on the shore of this black river, always drawn into its passing torrent.

## Chapter Six

# In the American Tradition
# (Solo Faces)

*Solo Faces* (1979) had a different kind of genesis than Salter's other novels in that it began as a screenplay, and the impetus for writing it in both forms came from others. Robert Redford, who had liked Salter's work on the film *Downhill Racer,* approached the writer in 1977 and engaged him to do a script about mountain climbing. Salter, like Redford an avid skier, welcomed the opportunity to explore a sport that required courage as well as skill and routinely offered opportunities for heroism. He immersed himself in climbing lore and took up the sport himself in an effort to understand it from the inside, a necessity given his belief that the best fiction is made from experience. "Every writer I know and admire," Salter said in the *Paris Review* interview, "has essentially drawn from his own life or his knowledge of things in life" ("Art," 61). He did his first climbing in Chamonix in heavy shoes and borrowed pants and quickly latched onto the lingo and gear of the sport. Despite his initial anguish and uncertainty, Salter, at 52 years old, soon climbed a number of peaks in the Alps, including the Index, the Aiguille Verte, the Arête de Cosmic, and the Floria. Back in the States, he met Royal Robbins, one of America's most prominent climbers, and climbed with him in Yosemite and the Rockies. In an *Esquire* article, Salter describes one of these climbs, an ascent of Monitor Rock, which is rated an imposing 5.8 in degree of difficulty (the range is from 5.0 to 5.13).[1] Although Salter always brought along pencil and paper on his climbs, he never managed to jot anything down. Instead, what climbing gave him was the confidence to write about the mountain predicament from the climber's perspective. He captures this perspective succinctly in the last lines of the *Esquire* piece: "Above, in the darkness is the summit. The rest is silence, stars, and the promise of triumph when day comes, a triumph more pure, more imperishable, more meaningless than almost anything else" ("Victory," 197). Salter's firsthand experience did not include an ascent of the Dru, which is the peak featured in the novel, although he speculates that he might have done a moderate route up the south face "given the right conditions and companion" ("Victory," 197). Although Salter has not climbed for some time, his son James Owen, who lives in Phoenix, remains an avid climber despite a rockfall accident that caused a permanent foot injury.

*Solo Faces* is based loosely on the life of Gary Hemming, an American who climbed in the 1950s and 1960s in California, New York, Wyoming, and the Alps and who became famous in France as the tight-lipped enigmatic hero who led a daring rescue on the Dru. Hemming ended his own life by gunshot in 1969 at Jenny Lake in the Tetons. Salter read Hemming's letters, researched his somewhat mysterious background, and came across a 10-minute interview with him that appeared on French television. It was the interview, revealing the compelling straightforwardness of the man, that convinced Salter Hemming was the right stuff of legend and inspired the portrait of his fictional Vernon Rand. Rand's companion and rival, John Cabot, was also based on a real climber, John Harlan, who later died on an ascent of the Eiger.

Salter wrote the screenplay, but Redford passed on the film project, perhaps because he did not see himself clearly in either role or perhaps because, as he once savvily acknowledged to Salter, "My presence in something . . . is enough to give it an aura of artificiality" (*BD*, 236). It would have died there, another of Salter's scripts denied animation like the six characters in Pirandello's famous play, had not Robert Emmett Ginna, Salter's good friend and then editor in chief at Little, Brown, offered him $50,000 to turn the story into a novel. Salter did just that, recasting the series of events and adding details necessary to fill out the plot and give greater dimension to the characters, and the book was finished in less than a year.

In attempting a novel about mountains and climbers, Salter had no eminent precedents. As George Pokorny reported in 1979, the year *Solo Faces* was published, "[A]lmost every appraisal of mountaineering literature states that the best works are the factual accounts of mountaineering achievements, and virtually all fiction is regarded as an alpine disaster."[2] Fiction's proclivity to disaster, according to Pokorny, derives from the novelist's dilemma of writing either in the technical jargon of the mountains and appealing only to a small number of climbers who enjoy fiction, or writing in the vernacular of the mass audience, thus losing authenticity. Although I have no doubt novelists have been hooked on the horns of this dilemma, I believe it to be based on a false assumption that the recesses of any esoteric experience cannot be communicated except through the technical language of that specialized realm. *The*

*New Yorker* over the years has demonstrated the falsity of this premise by its successful articles on subjects ranging from nuclear disarmament to space exploration, from Wittgenstein's philosophy to book publishing. The resources of language are infinite; the work involved in mining those resources, however, is forbidding enough for the indolent to be impaled on one of Pokorny's equally unsuccessful alternatives. Yet the best literature of mountaineering is no more written for mountaineers than was Hemingway's *The Old Man and the Sea* for fishermen.

*Solo Faces* not only illustrates the wrongness of Pokorny's assumption, but it sets a standard of writing that is useful in sifting away the mass of mountain writing from genuine mountain literature. Unburdened by jargon, the novel is authentic in its narration of mountain events while describing with very brief explanations such basic terms of climbing as pitons, belaying, and rappelling. More than that, however, the book sets itself apart from the stacks of books that use mountainous settings for the unfolding of plots essentially guided by other formulas—be they spy thrillers, detective stories, or political intrigues—and from scores of other novels that thinly disguise real-life adventure under the veneer of fiction. *Solo Faces* may be a "semi-biographical account of the rise and fall of the shadowy American Gary Hemming" as some reviewers noticed,[3] but Salter has taken this account and fashioned it into a tale of finely balanced proportions and set it squarely and honorably within the American literary tradition.

## In the American Tradition

Despite more recent formulations of this tradition, some even challenging that such a phenomenon exists, no one more cogently and convincingly traces the family tree than Richard Poirier in his *A World Elsewhere: The Place of Style in American Literature*. Poirier says that the major American writers from Emerson on have endeavored to oppose the forces of their environments by means of style. While he admits that one of the sustaining myths of all literature is that language can create environments radically different from those dictated by economic, political, and social systems, Poirier correctly claims that in America this myth is imbued with a sense of destiny derived from the successful settling and expanding of a previously hostile territory. Thus this tradition is inspired by the command of Emerson's Orphic poet to "Build therefore your own world," and thus American literature is full of images of the frontier. "Walden is the West for Thoreau. On the pond he can build an environment for himself in which not only wilderness but also the civilizing technologies are made subservient to him" (Poirier, 17).

Cooper, Emerson, Thoreau, Melville, Hawthorne, Twain, James—the classic American writers—"really do try," Poirier asserts, "against the perpetually greater power of reality, to create an environment that might allow some longer existence to the hero's momentary expansions of consciousness" (Poirier, 15). These special moments are rendered by the authors with all the authority and power that their styles can command. Why else, asks Poirier, do we remember most vividly passages that took only a few pages in a book of several hundred? Obviously these passages (an appropriate word) contain more of the author's heartfelt revelations than the overall structure of his work, which in most cases militates against and cancels out the luminous moments, for in most cases the authors are unable to resist the forces of the environment pressing in on their creations. Thus, for Poirier, *Huckleberry Finn* is the best history of American literature, summarizing in its pages the two forces that conflict throughout American literature, environment (the mainland and society) and vision (the river and the individual). Since eventually Huck goes back to civilization, environment does win out, but Poirier affirms it is these moments on the river that we remember most, that best carry the vision of Twain, and are the most meaningful parts of the book. It is easy to confirm Poirier's thesis with more examples than he cares to mention: the forest scenes in *The Scarlet Letter,* Bartleby's "I prefer not," Santiago's refusal to relinquish the blue marlin in *The Old Man and the Sea.* As Poirier states, "What we remember about a book or a writer—and this is notably true in American Literature—is often the smallest, momentary revelations that nonetheless carry, like the mystical experience to which William James alludes, an 'enormous sense of inner authority' " (Poirier, 14).

Poirier's identification of this tradition in American literature and his description of its characteristics are helpful in understanding the seriousness of context and the ambitiousness of *Solo Faces.* Using the central metaphor of the mountain, Salter has created a personal, romantic vision that challenges the ordinary environment of the society in which it exists. He presents us with still another American West, another frontier. And another hero who, like those of Poirier's canon, acts as a surrogate for the author in the central transcendent experiences of the book despite his ultimate absorption into the mundane everyday world. Salter's novel not only confirms the continued existence of this tradition, but it also throws light on a distinct, major branch not explored by Poirier.

If James Salter based his character Vernon Rand on the real-life American-in-France Gary Hemming, he did much more. In the quiet, enigmatic Rand, he has created a character as vivid and as unconventional as the heroes of *Walden* and *Huckleberry Finn*. Rand has no interest in and respect for the ordinary life of nine-to-five work with its houses, cars, families, and dogs. The mountains are to Rand what Walden Pond was to Thoreau and the river to Huck. After scaling the Dru, Rand is swept up in a passion for climbing: "When he climbed, life welled up, overflowed in him. His ambitions had been ordinary, but after the Dru it was different. A great, an indestructible happiness filled him. He had found his life. The back streets of town were his, the upper meadows, the airy peaks. It was the year when everything beckons, when one is finally loved."[4] Like Thoreau, who went to Walden so that when the time came to die he could not say that he had not lived and who found that life at Walden, Rand, moving past a long period in which he had defected from the climbing ranks, occupies the space that was meant to be his. And he does it like Thoreau, alone, for after his climb of the Dru with Cabot, "he left Chamonix by himself and for one reason or another began climbing that way" (*SF,* 131). His space is as rarefied as Thoreau's, for he occupies the heights of the Alps: "In the morning he woke among peaks incredibly white against the muted sky. There is something greater than the life of the cities, greater than money and possessions; there is a manhood that can never be taken away. For this, one gives everything."[5] This is the same manhood Emerson said in "Self-Reliance" that society was "in a conspiracy against."

Rand's possessions are as few as Thoreau's, and his physical needs, with the exception of sex, as simple: "He was famous, or nearly. There was a tent somewhere in the trees, where like a fugitive he had a few possessions, those he needed, rope strewn in dense coils at his feet, heaps of pitons, boots" (*SF,* 89). His lifestyle is consciously simple, lonely, and different. He "felt solitary, deep, like a fish in a river, mouth closed, uncaught, glistening against the flow" (*SF,* 91). Even in sex, his "love was the act of one person, it was not shared. He was like a man in a boat on a wide lake, a perfectly still lake at dawn" (*SF,* 103). And when he looked into the future Rand saw himself as unconventionally separate from society as ever: "He saw himself at forty, working for wages, walking home in the dusk. The windows of restaurants, the headlights of

cars, shops just being closed, all of it part of a world he had never sur-
rendered to, that he would defy to the end" (*SF,* 91).

Even more central to the American tradition delineated by Poirier
than the heroes' defiance of their worlds is the "eccentricity of defiance"
of the authors' styles. Poirier asserts that the classic American writers
seek through style to free their heroes temporarily from the entrapments
of time, nature, and society, from which ultimately there is no escape
(Poirier, 5). Salter's style is indeed a defiantly new thing, clean and pure
like Rand's climbing, unconventional in its use of sentence fragments
and run-ons. The only style it resembles, even slightly, is Hemingway's,
a resemblance not an imitation, which is why it works so well, why the
reviews of the novel singled it out for praise. No Hemingway imitator
has been able to get away with it because Hemingway's style was so
mannered that any imitation unconsciously lapsed into parody. Salter's
language exhibits the same grace and clarity of simple physical deeds
and elemental experiences that became distilled into the classic Hemingway style, but the differences are many. For one thing, Salter is not
biblically repetitive or liturgically incantatory with simple words as is
Hemingway. For another, Salter uses more active verbs, fewer dummy
subjects, and he relies less on a few reductive adjectives.

According to Poirier, only in certain passages of a novel does the
author take full visionary possession of a new land, different from the
environment pressing in on him. Poirier traces this inorganic method of
creation to Emerson's concern for the transcendent and the extraordinary, suggesting that in the best American writers, "the most engaging
elements of a book are usually those not coherent with the rest. In
Emerson's view writing is valuable for the stimulations offered locally,
by particular moments of the reading experience, and not for any retro-
spective consideration of the whole" (Poirier, 90–91).

Emerson's description fits *Solo Faces,* for the general movement of the
book is a downward one, with the hero, Rand, at the end vulnerable to a
sudden loss of confidence in his climbing, unsuccessful in trying to effect
by sheer willpower a recovery in his friend and rival Cabot, and aim-
lessly drifting from one menial job to another, unable even to affirm
anything of lasting value in his former halcyon days in the mountains.
Despite this rather tragic movement (not as tragic as the suicide of
Rand's model, Gary Hemming), the book's most memorable passages
are those during and right after Rand's two great climbs, the first with
Cabot, the second involving his rescue of the Italians. On the Dru,
Cabot's head has been smashed by falling rock and he appears doomed.

Somehow Rand manages to get him to a ledge and after spending the night there, Cabot convinces his partner that he is well enough to continue on to the top. During that day, they come to an exposed wide slab with holds so slight they were "hardly more than scribed lines" (*SF,* 81). Rand crosses first, and when Cabot is only a third of the way across, his belief gives way. He tells Rand to leave him, go on, and come back for him later:

> "I can't," Rand said. "Look, come on," he said casually. He was afraid of panic in his voice. He did not look down, he did not want to see anything. There is a crux pitch, not always the most technically difficult, where the mountain concedes nothing, not the tiniest movement, not the barest hope. There is only a line, finer than a hair, that must somehow be crossed.
>
> The emptiness of space was draining his strength from him, preparing him for the end. He was nothing in the immensity of it, without emotion, without fear and yet there was still an anguish, an overwhelming hatred for Cabot who hung there unwilling to move. Don't give up here, he was thinking. He was willing it, don't give up!
>
> When he looked, Cabot had taken another step. (*SF,* 81–82)

Rand's insistence, his perseverance, and his willpower are all triumphant over the dread inertia of despair. The two climbers drive to the top—now one, now the other encouraging, goading, and commanding—in a victory of one heart speaking to another and the other responding in kind. These are the charmed moments, and we exult in them with the hero and the author, exult in the triumph of will. The experience on the Dru is ultimately transforming, and when the pair return to Chamonix, "Glory fell on them lightly like the cool of the evening itself" (*SF,* 87).

Only later does the full force of this transformation work its way into Rand's consciousness. It happens after he has met Catherin and they have just spent the night together:

> He lay in bed. A womanly smell still clung to it. He could hear footsteps elsewhere in the house, they seemed aimless. Opening and closing of doors. The empty cups were on the floor. As if it had suddenly started, he noticed the ticking of her clock. He felt luxurious. He took himself for granted, his legs, his sexual power, his fate. A consciousness that had faded came to life. It was like a film when the focus is blurred and shifting and all at once resolves; there leaps forth a hidden image, incorruptible, bright. (*SF,* 96)

Like a Joycean epiphany, this moment after sex and climbing brings a magical clarity to Rand's mind. And in telling it, Salter is as careful as a poet in choosing the right details: bed, womanly smell, footsteps, doors, cups, clock. Rand's supine position is an expression of contentment, the most relaxed possible. The lingering female scent recalls the sensuousness of the previous night and allows its spell to remain. The footsteps, a reminder that he is not alone, also imply that most people must be up in the morning and getting ready for work, but not Rand. The opening and closing of doors become emblems of the physical intimacy the couple have shared and will share, and as well, of the new door to self-clarity Rand is passing through. The most telling detail, Rand's hearing of the clock "as if it had suddenly started," signals that now out of the amorphous past of quiet desperation has emerged a definite present and promising future. It signifies the start of life and the importance of relationship; for what is time, according to the cosmologist, but the measure of motion? And motion can only be measured relative to something or someone else, in this case Catherin. Salter lists the things Rand then took for granted. His legs are the principal tools of his climbing. His sexual power underscores the importance of this night with Catherin as a part of and a channel for his self-realization, and it also foreshadows what will become the last hope for Rand later, namely the final one of his string of lovers. His fate, as mysterious solo scaler of the highest peaks, has suddenly materialized from nowhere. In fact, Rand has gone from climbing bum to the legendary tight-lipped American, the hidden image that all at once leaps forth like a film coming into focus, literally an epiphany. Rand discovers his deepest, truest self—that soul which Emerson believed to be the only way to the divine—in this image of a man willing to challenge the impossible and still not boast of it.

For a climb to go down in memory, it must not only be extraordinarily difficult but inspired, "a line that led past a mere summit" (*SF,* 64). And it must also be recognized. Rand and Cabot's pioneering direct line up the Dru's West Face certainly met the first criterion. They are also fortunate that a famous climbing writer from a Geneva newspaper happened to be in the area at the time of their ascent and interviewed them afterward. Had it not been for his recognition, his stamp of authenticity on their endeavor, their climb might have been as unnoticed as a tree falling in the forest without observers. With him there, the aura of their achievement was sure to live on. When Salter writes, "The climb was one thing, its confirmation by such a man was another," one cannot help but relate the sentiment to writing as well (*SF,* 86). Salter knows well that for lasting fame, one must have confirmation by names who matter.

After the climb with Cabot and before Rand's brilliant rescue of the Italians, Salter has inserted a marvelous short scene that predicts his hero's less than glorious end. Situated between Rand's two great moments, it is an example of the author's ability to change tones and of his careful structuring of the novel. Rand and Catherin have gone to Paris where they meet Françoise (a friend of Catherin's) and Michel. It is Michel who impishly tells the story of an acquaintance who began to climb the most difficult peaks in Europe, dreaming of becoming the greatest climber of all time. Sensing Rand's interest, Michel says that the man had a greater inner strength than anyone he knew. "But," he continues, "something had changed in him, I could see it in his face. He had done everything and he was still unhappy. Two weeks ago . . ." As Michel breaks off, we are told that "Rand's heart was pounding. The panes of illusion were slipping from his life. He felt himself disappearing" (*SF,* 108). As Michel finishes telling them that the climber fell to his death on an easy climb, the women are angry and Rand sits in stunned silence. Like a prisoner, he has heard his sentence read. He recognizes the poetic truth of Michel's tale regardless of its literalness, and he knows it holds a lesson for him.

Rand returns to Chamonix and after a number of daring solo climbs reaches his apotheosis in leading a rescue team up the Dru direct to save two Italian climbers. When his party is caught in a slanting snowstorm by two in the afternoon, Rand "looked up to find the way. In his worn clothes and gauntness he appeared to be a secondary figure, someone in the wake of failed campaigns. It did not matter. He would do it. He was not merely making an ascent. He was clinging to the back of this monster. He had his teeth in the great beast" (*SF,* 143). They are successful, and later down below, Rand "let his glass be filled and relived the climb. Afterward he slept at Remy's. He slept as he had the first time long ago, as if all the earth were his and the night his chamber. He slept untroubled, with swollen hands" (*SF,* 150). Salter's style is spare, but like a painter he selects the right objects for his canvas. And it is precisely in such passages as those preceding that his style works to stretch the duration and expand the importance of those brief triumphal moments, which will not last. In these passages, his style attempts to free the hero "from the pressures of time . . . and from the social forces which are ultimately the undoing of American heroes and quite often of their creators" (Poirier, 5).

In Rand's case it is less the social forces and more the pressures of time, resistance of nature, and fading of his own will that bring about his undoing. One day, on a solo attempt of the Walker Spur, he simply gives in to the mountain and turns back, recognizing that "something had gone out of him" (*SF,* 179). Later, back in America, he looks in the mirror at a face "he once would have scorned," knowing that "he was suddenly too old." He had passed "the life of which he was the purest exemplar, which he would not spoil" (*SF,* 212). Although we see Rand at the end older, more somber, and certainly past his days of glory, at least he has the instinct for greatness to avoid swelling "the rout / Of lads that wore their honours out," men "whom renown outran / And the name died before the man."[6]

The book does end with two hopeful signs. One is the woman, now the fifth or sixth Rand has been with during the events of the novel, to whom he offers himself as a secure hold, telling her to "hold on" and "Don't get scared" (*SF,* 220). For the two of them he sees something possible, "there in the darkness, not a vision, not a sign, but a genuine shelter if he can only reach it" (*SF,* 220). Since Salter met and began living with Kay Eldredge not long before conceiving the story of *Solo Faces,* this may have influenced his interpretation of what Gary Hemming lacked in taking his own life. He gives Rand the "genuine shelter" that Hemming apparently did not have. The other positive note is the perdurance of the legend Rand has left by disappearing. "They talked of him . . . which was what he had always wanted" (*SF,* 213). In fact, by his not writing Cabot or keeping in touch with the climbing world, Rand's renown grows. Now he is seen in Colorado, now California. His pure ideal of climbing lives on. He enters "the legend he was already part of" (*SF,* 212). It remains uncorrupted and mysterious. Salter tells us, "The acts themselves are surpassed but the singular figure lives on. . . . Rand had somehow succeeded. He had found the great river. He was gone" (*SF,* 213). Like Huck Finn, Rand is defeated at last by being submerged into the realities of ordinary life, but the moments of his freedom and transcendence on the mountain remain in the minds of the reader as surely as Huck's freedom on the river. Rand the legend lives on in the same way the other defiant heroes of American literature live on.

## Two Strands of the Tradition

When Richard Poirier asserts that the building of a house or dynasty is a crucial metaphor for the American stylistic tradition he has traced so ingeniously in *A World Elsewhere,* he is correctly locating part of the tradition, but not all of it. Poirier uses Thoreau's Walden as his founding example of "something like an obsession in American literature with plans and efforts to build houses, to appropriate space to one's desires, perhaps to inaugurate therein a dynasty that shapes time to the dimensions of personal and familial history" (Poirier, 14). The other examples Poirier offers from Hawthorne, James, Faulkner, and Fitzgerald are apt illustrations of the metaphor. Poirier, however, seems to imply that the image fits the whole tradition with which he is dealing, when in fact another metaphor is of equal importance and better describes the other half of the tradition. Whitman, Dickinson, Melville, half of Thoreau, Twain, Hemingway, and now Salter establish as their ruling image not a house (hero as builder) or a dynasty (hero as founder, patriarch), but a nomad, an individual so estranged from the realities of the world that he or she will not or cannot settle down and take a place in that world.

Another novel about a climbing situation that was written about the same time as *Solo Faces,* Charles Gaines's *Dangler* (1980), helps clarify the two distinct symbolic situations. Eric Dangler builds a camp in New Hampshire for rich adults to experience the challenges of the primitive under the instruction and protection of the owner himself, assuring the campers controlled victories over natural obstacles. Dangler's project is as immense as his fortune and imagination. His campers climb rock faces, canoe white water, and shoot wild boar, but the ultimate test is a winter climb up a New Hampshire mountain. Dangler intends to start a new society, one that will allow the human race to recapture that primitive strength which enabled it to survive thus far. Like Thoreau, Dangler believes that people are infinitely adaptable to circumstances and that in confronting the elemental challenges of nature individuals can remake themselves into better, stronger, more noble beings. The camp is a tangible symbol of Dangler's intention to form the new community, foremost among whom is his friend from college Andrew Cobb. It is to this group that Dangler bequeaths his vision, even though he dies in the final climb and his great house, Wildwood, burns. The novel's jacket tells us that it was Gaines's intent to create a character as emblematic of America as Jay Gatsby, an intent at least partially executed by embodying the dreams of the protagonist in the image of the house he has built. "No one," says Dangler is "more American than I."[7]

Both *Solo Faces* and *Dangler* are in the American tradition of creating a personal, romantic vision to challenge the ordinary environment in which their heroes live. Rand and Dangler both have qualities of vision and will beyond the usual: Rand, when he is free and easy in the mercy of his glory, capable of responding to and surmounting almost any obstacle; Dangler, when he realizes that Wildwood is something that people need because it provides the confrontations with nature necessary to wipe away the softening comforts of civilization. Both books are tragedies of sorts, for in both environment conquers vision: Rand drifts off at the end, incapable of finally proving the superhuman power of his will by getting Cabot to walk, his nerves no longer of the mountain variety; Dangler dies and Cobb afterward reflects bitterly on the emptiness of the man's dream, its essential craziness. Yet Gaines wants it both ways, for Cobb has been transformed by his meeting the test of heroism on the mountain; and the memories of passages similar to the ones noted in *Solo Faces* linger in the mind after reading *Dangler* as well. So while Cobb consciously blames Dangler for merely "pursuing fantasies of himself" (Gaines, 276), Cobb's own life has been changed by the experience. On the mountain he had felt that "his entire life had been a preparation for this moment" (Gaines, 261). And Dangler's exhortation to Cobb at the crucial point, "part of everything that made us durable is in you," is as much a celebration of the human will and fellowship as was Rand's urging of Cabot on the Dru (Gaines, 265). Something of the intuitive rightness and charm of Rand the climber and the powerful determination of Dangler the builder remains in the dust of their respective tragedies.

Rand and Dangler assume radically different postures of opposition to the world about them. Dangler builds an enclave, a fortress in which his chosen few followers can live a lifestyle counter to that of their surroundings. His camp is clearly an execution of Emerson's poetic injunction to "build your own world." Thus does Wildwood take its place in the list of examples that show the "obsession in American literature with plans and efforts to build houses" (Poirier, 17). Although the novel is not up to its illustrious predecessors' achievements, Eric Dangler's camp has the same symbolic intent as Thoreau's cabin and Gatsby's estate.

By contrast, Vernon Rand is an absolute nomad. From the first events of the novel to the last, he never occupies any space that he can rightfully call his own. For Rand "what mattered was to be a part of existence, not to possess it" (*SF,* 132). Rented rooms, countryside sheds, mountain bivouacs, and the houses of others provide him temporary shelter. Mircea Eliade explains the symbolic import of this nomadic stance in ancient societies: "If possessing a house implies having assumed a stable situation in the world, those who have renounced their houses, the pilgrims and ascetics, proclaim by their desire to leave the world, their refusal of any worldly situation."[8] When this image of nomad is combined with the activity of solo climbing, as in Rand's case, the symbolic structure points all the more to a "refusal of any worldly situation" and reaffirms the moments of transcendence expressed in the passages previously cited. This posture contrasts sharply with that of the house builder, who in primitive societies, Eliade explains, symbolizes the creation of the world, establishing an absolute around which all other things can be related and hence validated. Both symbolic stances can be used to express opposition to the environment. In fact, the tradition of defiance in American literature traced by Richard Poirier is really a dual tradition of builders and nomads, exemplified by *Dangler* and *Solo Faces*.

Even the effort of the American authors to oppose their environment through the medium of style can be viewed in two lights. It is, of course, possible to say with Poirier that style is the world writers build to hold back the forces of environment. But it is equally possible to view style as the fluid movement of the artist's vision, avoiding the set behavior and standard roles imposed on the hero by the world of the novel. In fact, this latter view of style as movement fits well the "special passages" effect that Poirier observes in the American writers. If the authors accomplish their purposes by means of momentary revelations that can like "mystical experience" confer an "enormous sense of inner authority," are not these passages suited by the metaphor of "movement" better than the metaphor of "construction"?

James Salter's *Solo Faces,* then, not only takes its place in the major tradition of American literature but also, through the nomadic stance of its hero, helps to clarify a significant branch of that tradition. Vernon Rand walks in the footsteps of such unrooted wanderers as Captain Ahab, Huck Finn, and Jake Barnes. *Solo Faces* is a novel finely crafted in style and structure and carefully thoughtful in its exploration of the sunlit moments and twilight hours of a great mountain climber.

## Reviews and Assessment

It is understandable, but not particularly helpful, that a number of reviewers called *Solo Faces* a macho novel. Mountain climbing, even 20 years after the novel was written, remains largely a male sport, although there are certainly women who have pursued mountain challenges with the same visionary single-mindedness that has driven legions of men to risk everything—relationships, family ties, and domestic responsibilities—to reach the summit. Salter's hero, Rand, belongs with this number, singular only in his ability and conviction. The following passage from the novel, explaining Rand's power, was cited by Peter Prescott in *Newsweek* as evidence of the novel's machismo: "There are men who seem destined to always go first, to lead the way. They are confident in life, they are the first to go beyond it. Whatever there is to know, they learn before others. Their very existence gives strength and drives one onward" (*SF,* 144). It seems to me what Salter is describing here is the quality of leadership that has discovered new continents, settled lands, made medical and scientific breakthroughs, raised skyscrapers, waged wars, and ruled nations. In the world of any sport or endeavor like mountain climbing, these leaders rise like cream, and because they have been in the course of things mostly men, Salter's statement reflects that. It is clearly not intended to exclude the relatively few women who have led others to the heights. Rather than exhibit machismo, his words seem rather to describe a genuine phenomenon, great leadership.

Part of the macho allegation stems from what Prescott caricatures as the role women are reduced to in the book: "A woman is a smooth-skinned primate who, by virtue of her domesticity and enervating sexuality, is incapable of understanding a man's need to blaze his solitary path in a senseless world."[9] In a similar vein Peter Wolfe wrote in *Saturday Review,* "The women in the book exist merely to provide sex for their climber-lovers and then to be dropped."[10] Since these are serious and not uncommon misreadings of the novel, they must be addressed.

Of course, Rand is male, and the greater part of the book takes a male perspective, expressing his attitudes. And, although he is a hero, Rand is no saint, nor is he judged as one by Salter. It should not shock or surprise us that Rand, who is incurably nomadic, leaves a number of women strewn in his path. When he jumps from the bed of Colette into the arms of Simone, Salter writes, "One woman is like another. Two are like another two. Once you begin there is no end" (*SF,* 156). What these lines imply is that once one woman has been left for another, the same thing will happen again. Once in the current, the same forces will tug one along. Of course, it is Rand's attitude, not the novel's or Salter's, and we must remember that Rand himself looks back on this time in Paris as nearly ruinous to himself, spoiled by fame and women who desired him, willing to live off them and his instincts for pleasure. When Banning tells Rand, "It couldn't have ruined you," Rand answers, "It came close" (*SF,* 168).

Prescott's and Wolfe's allegations simply do not hold up under scrutiny. For one thing the women come off rather well in the novel.

Contrary to Prescott's observation, they really do understand Rand's need to climb. In fact, it is part of his attraction. Rand's lovers "were witnesses. . . . They were the bearers of his story, scattered throughout the world" (*SF*, 162). And Catherin, after she has been left by Rand in his refusal of the responsibilities of fatherhood, writes to him: "I know you have glory waiting for you" (*SF*, 173). Furthermore, the women more than hold their own in relation to Rand. When he is stupid and unfaithful, Salter gives full voice to the betrayed lover, Simone, who chastises him: "When someone trusts you, you mean you don't feel any regret if you betray them? Going from woman to woman, from place to place like a dog in the street, that fulfills you? The hero with gorgeous ideals, beautiful ideals, you turn your back for a minute and he sleeps with your friend. It's disgusting" (*SF*, 159). And Catherin, whose love almost held Rand, is totally superior to him when he returns ostensibly to see their son but secretly to learn if anything remained between them. Nothing does, and she dismisses him from the second-floor window with one word, "Goodbye."

Actually whatever macho sentiments Rand expresses about women as incidental and climbing as the ultimate test of courage are subverted by the course of the novel's plot. Rand comes to realize his limitations in his own failures, of courage on the Walker and of leadership in his inability to inspire Cabot to walk after Cabot's accident. He is a victim like the other heroes in American literature. He is defeated by time and nature itself, which is not susceptible to the power of will, and by the inner corrosion of his own motives. He acknowledges to Banning before his solo attempt of the Walker that what he is really interested in is "making people envious—that's it. That's all it is. I wasn't always that way. There may have been a tendency but not much. I was stronger" (*SF*, 172). Given this corruption of the purity of his motives, it is no surprise that he loses courage on the ascent. As he says afterward, "I didn't prepare . . . that was the trouble. I wasn't ready. I lacked the courage" (*SF*, 179).

The novel's ending is the ultimate refutation of Prescott's and Wolfe's charges of male chauvinism. Once again Salter gives Rand's lover, now Paula, a powerful voice when she tells him, "I want to trust someone. . . . I want to feel something. With you, though, it's like somehow it goes into empty air." Rand responds using the same language of his climbing triumphs on the Dru: "Well, what you have to do is hold on. . . . Don't get scared" (*SF*, 200). This is significant because Rand, by using the climbing trope, has transferred its importance to the realm of relationship. His final injunction, "to hold on," suggests that one can triumph in relationships only by the same tenaciousness needed on a climb. Having realized through his dissipation in Paris and through his failure to rescue Cabot from his paralysis that mountain success does not automatically lead to success in other parts of life, Rand continues to search for connections between climbing and life. He finds one here in his recognition of relationship as a climbing tandem. "He sees it there in the darkness, not a vision, not a sign, but a genuine shelter" (*SF,* 220). Rand and Paula's holding onto one another will create a shelter against the threatening elements. These words and Rand's final vision of Paula and himself together inside such a shelter with the rain falling around them indicate a hopeful transformation that belies Prescott's and Wolfe's reading of the novel.

Two reviews of the novel stand out above the rest for their perceptivity. In the *New York Times Book Review,* novelist Vance Bourjaily thought the book "a beautifully fashioned and satisfying novel . . . not so much about mountain climbing as of a man obsessed with the sport."[11] Bourjaily reads the story as a writer, noting particularly Salter's "rhetorical control" as he describes minor characters in "a resourcefully elliptical way" and even shifts effectively to their point of view. He cites an example from the Dru rescue when we share the viewpoint of Dennis, one of the less-experienced climbers: "All that allowed him to go on, all that preserved him from panic, was a kind of numbness, an absolute concentration on every hold and a faith complete, unthinking, in the tall figure above" (*SF,* 143). And later, "Dennis had outclimbed his fear. An exhilaration that was almost dizzying came over him. He was one of them, he was holding his own" (*SF,* 144). As Bourjaily notes, since we have already scaled the Dru with Rand, "[I]t is refreshing to make the second ascent with someone quite different" (Bourjaily, 11). Bourjaily also points to one scene where the switching of viewpoints causes some confusion, a strange encounter in which Rand uses a gun to try and rouse Cabot out of his paralysis.

Another review, by Francis King in the *Spectator,* deserves to be read in full. King identifies part of Salter's unique accomplishment when he says, "I can think of no novel that comes closer to explaining the nature of [mountain climbing's] mystique."[12] King recognizes that "Rand lives shamelessly on women" and "no less shamelessly . . . swaps one woman for another," but he places Rand's conduct within the context of his extraordinary talent, noting that Rand's "mountaineering gift is akin to a gift for music or mathematics—it is independent of any distinction in any other sphere of life." Following this line of thinking, King notes that "the single mindedness with which Rand sets out on his lonely conquests is a potent metaphor of the artistic vocation. Climbing and the highest artistic achievement demand a similar ruthlessness both with self and with others; and in each the aspirant may suffer an inexplicable loss of nerve or of inspiration, so that in a moment he plunges from the airiest heights to the darkest depths" (King, 22).

King is right. Part of the mystique of mountaineering at its highest level is esthetic, the right ascent, inspired and dramatically simple, the direct. And the whole enterprise of climbing in the novel becomes a metaphor for artistic creation—difficult, at times nearly impossible, susceptible to sudden failures of nerve, but in the end glorious and monumental. "In its great moments," says Salter, "climbing is an ordeal, and like most ordeals it has the power to bind one to it closely. When it is all over, you remember the triumphs, but they are broad, like happiness" ("Victory," 195). It is to Salter's credit that he has written a book whose lines have the beauty of an original ascent. His celebration of the sunlit triumphs of an American hero who is finally defeated by the forces of time and nature is a worthy addition to the venerable tradition of the American novel.

# Chapter Seven
## Short Story Writer
## (Dusk and Other Stories)

More than a decade after the publication of his initial novel, Salter's short story "Am Strand von Tanger" appeared in the pages of the *Paris Review* (Fall 1968). He had written a few stories before, but this was admittedly his first one of any merit, and it was the first to be accepted in print. George Plimpton, editor of the review since its founding in 1953 by young Americans Peter Matthiessen and Harold Humes, had published *A Sport and a Pastime* under the *Paris Review* imprint, so the quarterly—which by 1968 had distinguished itself with its fiction, poetry, and interviews—seemed an ideal placement for Salter's early stories, which dealt with Americans living or traveling in Europe. Of the five stories that Salter published between 1968 and 1972, four appeared in the review. The only exception was "Cowboys" (later retitled "Dirt"), which somehow found its way to the *Carolina Quarterly*.

Then for nine years Salter turned away from the short story, concentrating instead on film scripts and his two novels *Light Years* and *Solo Faces*. He did not return to the form until 1981 when *Grand Street*, a new literary quarterly founded by Ben Sonnenberg, featured Salter's story "Akhnilo" in its autumn issue. During the 1980s short story writing and journalism were Salter's major occupations. He wrote a half dozen stories, distributing their initial placements equally between *Esquire*, whose fiction editor Rust Hills admired Salter's work, and *Grand Street*, whose editor in chief Sonnenberg had first become acquainted with Salter through a play the latter had submitted to Lincoln Center, where Sonnenberg had been a reader.

When Salter resumed writing stories again in the early 1980s, he did not have a collection in mind. At the urging, however, of North Point Press, which reissued *Light Years* (1982) and *A Sport and a Pastime* (1985) in elegant sewn softcover editions on acid-free paper, he began to consider such a collection. And when he had enough material, North Point issued *Dusk and Other Stories* (1988) in a hardcover edition with a lovely cover photograph by Yvonne Jacquette of the East River and Brooklyn Bridge at dusk. The reviews were overwhelmingly positive, and the book garnered the P.E.N./Faulkner Award for its author in 1989, his most prestigious prize thus far.

The short story form was a natural for Salter, who has always liked brevity and whose novels are shaped and polished with poetic sensibility. Of the many writers of short fiction he has admired—among them Colette, Céline, de Montherlant—none rank higher than Anton Chekhov and Isaac Babel. Although he did not discover Babel until 1975, after he had written both *A Sport and a Pastime* and *Light Years,* he was astonished by Babel's brilliant and unsentimental style: "Every sentence is like an arrow thudding into a target, and Babel is stunningly succinct. His famous dictum states that no iron can pierce the human heart so chillingly as a period put in exactly the right place."[1] Babel also was heroic in his artistic commitment, working endlessly on manuscripts: "There was a trunk full of them that just disappeared with work in it that he simply wasn't ready to have printed yet" ("Art," 86).

Salter himself works on manuscripts for a long time. The initial delivery date for his memoir, *Burning the Days* (1997), was 1989. He does not write every day partly because of the need to take care of other matters and partly because he must first have a sense of readiness and anticipation before taking up the pen. When he is writing, he likes the process of rubbing words together and searching for their electric potential. He will spend hours on a single paragraph. The time it took him to write some of his stories is out of all proportion to their length. In 1986 he reported working on a story, "every day realizing it was becoming worse and worse. Became inexplicably ill-tempered. This morning however with the skies blown clean and blue air I read it skimmingly again and to my surprise saw a few redeeming things. I'm going to make one more effort. It's called TWENTY MINUTES, takes about ten to read and will have taken months to write."[2] He does his first drafts longhand in a script that is meticulously well formed and clear. His letters are smallish and shaped with the precision of an artist or accountant. He types this version, makes corrections that are lucid and exact, retypes, corrects, and retypes. He does not use a computer. The act of making corrections by hand on a typed text is for him part of the tactile sensation of writing. A page from one of his typescripts with his penned corrections gives evidence of many skirmishes fought and won in his ceaseless battle to make language serve the moment.

## Early Stories

Salter's first story, "Am Strand von Tanger," like *A Sport and a Pastime,*
tells of an American youth abroad; in the story he is an aspiring artist
living in Barcelona. The image of the developing artist dominates
Salter's early short fiction, appearing in three other stories published in
the *Paris Review:* "The Cinema" (Summer 1970), "The Destruction of
Goetheanum" (Winter 1971), and "Via Negativa" (Fall 1972)—all in
*Dusk.* Together his *Paris Review* stories constitute Salter's "Portrait of the
Artist as a Young Man," although clearly their themes are not exclusively about art. In each of the stories the young male protagonist has a
desire for greatness and a need to have the image of his greatness confirmed by someone else, a woman. Aside from this, each version of the
artist differs.

Malcolm in "Am Strand von Tanger" is more involved with the idea
of being an artist than with craft; he is "preparing for the arrival of that
great artist he one day expects to be, an artist in the truly modern sense
which is to say without accomplishments but with the convictions of
genius" (*D,* 5). Although thus far unaccomplished, Malcolm, like other
artist figures in Salter's fiction and like the author himself, is moved by
exemplars. He is living in Barcelona because of a story by Paul Morand
and because it was Antonio Gaudi's city, where he lived and left his
unfinished cathedral. Like the cathedral, Malcolm is "a process not fully
complete" (*D,* 5). To confirm his conviction of genius, he needs but a
single follower, which he has in Nico, with whom he "is deep in the currents of a slow, connubial life" (*D,* 5). The story reveals how quickly and
surely such a life can be disrupted when the couple one Sunday go to the
beach with Inge, Nico's old roommate, who steals Malcolm's attention
and shatters Nico's confidence by her offhand sexuality and cynicism.
The supplanting of Nico in Malcolm's feelings, her defeat, is reflected in
the fate of her parrot, which they find dead on returning, just as Nico is
now dead in Malcolm's affection. Just the previous week the couple's
other bird died, "[s]uddenly. He wasn't even sick" (*D,* 8). Such sudden,
irreversible changes in relationships occur throughout Salter's stories.

Although "Am Strand von Tanger" was Salter's first story, the writing
is assured from the outset: "Barcelona at dawn. The hotels are dark. All
the great avenues are pointing to the sea" (*D,* 3). The spare lines create a
sense of timeless universality that is fostered by an absence of references
to dated events in the story. The figure of Inge is drawn with swift, sure
strokes from her first arrival at the apartment "in a camel skirt and a

blouse with the top buttons undone" (*D,* 6). Salter also showed that he could end a story effectively. Nico is in bed with Malcolm, her back to him, sobbing over her dead bird. He notices her small breasts and large behind. He thinks of her father's three secretaries (undoubtedly connected to Inge's earlier statement that a man needs more than one woman). And his final thought is "Hamburg is close to the sea," a sign of his new inclinations, for Inge is from Hamburg. As he did in *A Sport and a Pastime,* Salter in his portrait of Malcolm captures the sense one had at a certain age that anything was possible in love or deed. The situation is timeless, but it reminds me of a young Hemingway being led from the arms of Hadley into those of her friend Pauline Pfeiffer.

The picture of backstage life on a European film shoot that "The Cinema" presents clearly draws on Salter's screen-writing foray in the 1960s. Writing for the movies proved profitable but artistically unsatisfying for Salter. When asked why he eventually gave it up, he replied, "That life was not for me" (Letter, 1992). It is easy to see what he meant by "that life" from "The Cinema," which mildly satirizes most of those connected with the film being made: vain actors and actresses who believe their screen roles, producers scandalously ignorant of film history, and a director who must manipulate by subterfuge, flattery, and bravado. Set in Rome, the story offers several variations on the artist, revealing whole histories, whole worlds in Salter's deft sleight of hand. The leading actor Guivi is now basking in what he feels to be the glorious height of his career at 37, in the midst of an affair with his beautiful costar—"love scenes during the day, he thought wearily, love scenes at night" (*D,* 87). Although "he had a moment on the screen that would never be forgotten," Guivi, we learn, has no talent, and his career is already in decline although he is unaware of it. "Within three years his career would be over. He would see himself in the flickering television as if it were some curious dream" (*D,* 87). The director works like a dynamo, maintaining optimism even though he knows it is rubbish. His real goal is productivity: "Two films a year, he repeated . . . that was the keystone of all his belief" (*D,* 86).

The foremost image of the artist in the story, however, is the screenwriter Peter Lang, the author's alter ego. Like Salter, Lang had changed his name, from Lengsner; and like Salter, his main concern is with his craft. In fact, Lang's concept for his film script aptly describes Salter's own writing style: "Its power came from its chasteness, the discipline of images. It was a film of indirection, the surface was calm with the calm of daily life" (*D,* 76). Also like Salter, Lang hovers in the background of the film's making, without faith in the director or the process, caught up in something he cannot believe in. The story's ending is as daring as a high trapeze catch and flawless, with Lang receiving confirmation of his artistic vision in an oblique way. Eva, an Italian woman doing publicity on the film, has joined him for a quiet dinner and talk about their lives while the rest of the film crew attends a gala party. After dinner and some moments of intimacy in a parked car outside of town, they separate. The next morning she telephones him while he is still in bed and reads part of an article about a lonely astronomer who in 1868 discovered a new planet at the very time "the whole world of fashion" amused themselves at the party of the year thrown by the Prince of Milan. Eva's call shows her faith in Lang's talent and her belief that he must follow the example of the astronomer who worked alone while the princes feasted. As a result, Lang is transformed: "His ecstasy was beyond knowing. The roofs of the great cathedrals shone in the winter air" (D, 91). Within the course of the story, one can sense Salter discovering his own artistic path, away from the glitter of the cinema, guided by a woman's faith.

The artist in "The Destruction of Goetheanum" is Hedges, a writer with a grand design for a novel, as grand as the design of Rudolf Steiner, who outside Basel built an immense curved double-domed structure all of wood, called "The Goetheanum" after Goethe, his inspiration. Hedges is the artist staking everything on his *magnum opus* while "on every side it seemed, young men were writing film scripts or selling things for enormous sums" (D, 140). The issues here are the lineage of art (one generation's genius begetting the next), the necessity of belief in one's own gifts, and the needed confirmation of those gifts by another. Hedges is in Basel because it is only 40 miles from Dornach, where Steiner established his community and erected his masterpiece. To be there he has left his wife and children in New York and run away with Nadine, who is "the illusionist of Hedges' life" until, in the course of the story, she leaves. We are reminded at the story's end that Steiner's magnificent building burned to the ground, his creation now only a thing of memory, and we are left to imagine that the desertion of Nadine signals a like conflagration of Hedges's grand ambitions. Yet Salter clearly admires Hedges and his dramatic devotion, for "he was following the path of greatness which is the same as disaster, and he had the power to make one devote oneself to his life" (D, 135).

This story has another side as well. The whole history of Nadine and Hedges is refracted through the consciousness of an unnamed man who meets Nadine at a social in Basel and is fascinated by her and the possibilities opened by her now waning belief in Hedges. In the course of their conversations and meetings, he becomes entranced although she seems indifferent. Salter has a way of showing how individuals situate themselves toward others and the mysterious chemistry that can result. The story's central moment happens at dusk while the two are walking toward her hotel: "They stopped once, before a restaurant with a tank of fish, great speckled trout larger than a shoe lazing in green water, their mouths working slowly. Her face was visible in the glass like a woman's on a train, indifferent, alone. Her beauty was directed toward no one. She seemed not to see him, she was lost in her thoughts. Then, coldly, without a word, her eyes met his. They did not waver. In that moment he realized she was worth everything" (D, 139). Later, when Nadine has disappeared and he cannot find her, he recognizes that "there is always one moment . . . it never comes again" (D, 147). His moment had passed in that walk at dusk, and now he as well as Hedges has lost Nadine forever. This story is about the precariousness of both art and love. Although a mystery lingers at the end about Nadine's disappearance, its significance for Hedges seems clear, signaling the end of his grand illusions.

Similar issues of artistic achievement and intimacy appear in "Via Negativa" as we get two versions of the artist, both writers, one successful and the other failing, though more devoted. Nile is the latter, a minor writer with a single story published struggling to retain belief in himself somewhat like Hedges. He knows living writers and reveres dead ones, but he is now unable to produce, unable to face the truth of his own marginality, although his girlfriend, Jeanine, has already done so. The last element of Nile's failure occurs when Jeanine meets by chance the successful writer whom Nile has so envied and despised. She is drawn into an immediate intimacy with her new acquaintance by the tug of his prowess and that of the larger world he represents. In the hour of dusk Nile tears up her apartment in a rage over her abandonment of him, although he is ignorant of the depth of her apostasy. The title of the story, "Via Negativa," the traditional path of holiness through denial, suggests that Nile's road toward artistic sainthood is to be the hard way.

One could question Salter's reliance on coincidence in this story, the happenstance of Jeanine meeting P, the despised writer, while Nile is raging in her across-town apartment. It is, however, as though Salter were trying to say such unlikely events are also a part of life. And he anticipates the reader's wariness by proclaiming, just before Jeanine meets the writer, "All is chance or nothing is chance" (*D,* 130). "Via Negativa" is not one of Salter's best stories, but it does show Salter at this period in his life formulating an artistic credo in his stories. Sensing the lack of public confirmation of his own ability as a writer, Salter recognized the importance of those who did believe in him and the importance of keeping his goals and ambitions high and pure, guided by the example of dead writers whose achievements outstripped their contemporary fame. He also sensed how vital it was that, among the believers in his talent, there be a certain kind of woman, self-composed, intelligent, and totally independent in her beauty. These early stories show as well that Salter was acutely aware of how crucial a role unguarded moments play in chance meetings and extended love affairs.

The only Salter story of this early period not set in Europe or New York, not directly about artists, and not published in the *Paris Review* is "Dirt" (originally titled "Cowboys" in *Carolina Quarterly,* Spring 1971). Besides its southwestern setting, it is also unique for its flat tone and blue-collar characters. Although there are no artists as such, the grizzled American day laborer, Harry Mies, mixes concrete and pours foundations with the care of one. Readers glimpse Harry's life as it nears its end: the integrity of his work; the loyalty of his young helper, Billy; and the joy of the stories the old man likes to tell of California and days gone by. Lives, the tale implies, have a way of overlapping, each person's story impinging on others even among the most stoic of loners. Harry will one day be a legend like those in his tales. If the *Paris Review* stories picture the artist as a young man, "Dirt" presents an image of the aging craftsman, fulfilled not by the fame that seemed so crucial in the other stories about younger artists, but by the purity of his dedication to hard work, quality, and self-satisfaction. He will not die unknown but will live on in the memories and tales of those who worked with him, like his latest helper, Billy.

"Dirt" is placed last in *Dusk* because it is about the inevitable endings and hopeful continuations of life. The title reflects both the earth on which Billy is crawling at the outset and the earth in which Harry is laid to rest. Although this is the only early story whose protagonist has nothing to do with art, ironically Harry Mies is Salter's most compelling and enduring vision of the artist in his stories. Harry leaves little behind him except the results of his work, his well-worn instruments, and his tales—the perfect legacy, the only one worthy of our aspirations, according to Salter. Life whisks by and only stories and memories remain. The glory of Harry's work will live on in Billy. After Harry dies, Billy heads to Mexico with a local girl, and Salter concludes his collection with the sentence: "They told each other stories of their life" (*D,* 157). What else, he implies, is there?

## Later Stories

Six of the stories in *Dusk* were written during the course of the 1980s, with a decade's interval between them and the earlier stories. Three of these later stories deal with men's lives, three with women's. "Akhnilo" (1981) and "Lost Sons" (1983) focus on men confronting their pasts. In the case of Dartmouth graduate Eddie Fenn in "Akhnilo," the past means failure to follow his dreams and to make money. One evening he awakens to what he imagines to be the distant sounds of those dreams, great and mysterious, but it is too late. Summoned by a "sea of cries," Eddie slides trancelike out of his bedroom window and follows the sound to his barn, where he receives "a kind of signal, a code" (*D,* 106). When he returns to his bedroom, again by the unconventional rooftop approach, he struggles to hold the four words of this dream revelation in his mind, but he is drawn away from it by his wife and daughter's solicitous concern, suggesting that the domestic situation itself is incompatible with this dream: "The countless voices were receding, turning into silence" (*D,* 111). Fenn's family had once saved him from spiraling alcoholism, but this intervention was "not without cost" (*D,* 108), and when "he often woke at night, [his wife] would find him sitting in the kitchen, his face looking tired and old" (*D,* 110). The strange nighttime revelation culminates in Fenn's emotional breakdown, "nearly weeping as he tried to pull away" from his wife and daughter's ministrations.

This story was anthologized in *American Short Story Masterpieces,* edited by Raymond Carver and Tom Jenks, and it does have an eerie, mysterious, and unrealistic quality that reminds one of John Cheever's classic "The Swimmer." Salter's writing is flawless, exhibiting his gift for compressing years within sentences. He writes about Fenn's failure: "There was something quenched in him. When he was younger it was believed to be some sort of talent, but he had never really set out in life, he had stayed close to shore" (*D,* 105). And with a few images of the natural world Salter conveys how fragile is life: "That afternoon he had seen a robin picking at something near the edge of the grass, seizing it, throwing it in the air, seizing it again: a toad, its small, stunned legs fanned out. The bird threw it again. In ravenous burrows the blind shrews hunted ceaselessly, the pointed tongues of reptiles were testing the air, there was the crunch of abdomens, the passivity of the trapped, the soft throes of mating. His daughters were asleep down the hall. Nothing is safe except for an hour" (D, 106). The lines are stunning, capped by Salter's characteristic crystallization of all that has gone before, the precariousness of life's dreams, in a terse and telling final sentence. Apparently this sense of life's fragility was the cry at the heart of Eddie's revelation that so shattered him.

Ed Reemstma in "Lost Sons" (*Grand Street,* Winter 1983) returns to a reunion of his 1960 class at West Point, hoping to revise somehow his outcast standing, only to find the past is irreversible and that he still lives in its long shadow. Reemstma is a painter, but his art is a minor part of the story. Its only effect is to garner attention from a couple of his classmates' wives, and even that attention, the only redeeming moment of the weekend for him, is passing and polite. At one point, during the nominations for vacated class offices, Reemstma's name comes up, and he is tricked into thinking they are seriously proposing him only to learn it was a joke. "He felt as if he had been betrayed" (D, 101). The story ends with the awaited arrival of a class celebrity Klingbeil, who has the same nickname, "Hooknose," that was often used by one of Salter's classmates. The old game Reemstma's classmates begin playing reinforces what he sensed all along, he was never a part of the group and he never will be. As a picture of a typical college reunion, the story is economical and brilliant. Its tone is wistful, conveying both nostalgia for the past and resignation for its unchanged hierarchies. Although Reemstma is by no means Salter, one passage about Reemstma does capture how Salter came to embrace the military life: "How ardently he had believed in the image of a soldier. He had known it as a faith, he had clung to it dumbly, as a cripple clings to God" (D, 98).

The male characters in "American Express" (*Esquire,* February 1988), Salter's own favorite among his stories, are anything but failures or outcasts. Frank and Alan are lawyers and sons of lawyers, who have come down the fast track of success and are on holiday in Europe, eventually picking up an Italian schoolgirl. From the defining moment of their early career in the law, when they took a fortune-making case away from their firm only months before trial, the two have succeeded by inventing their own rules. The more daring one, Frank, slips easily into quid-pro-quo intimacy with an attractive client when she lacks the resources to employ him to renegotiate a divorce settlement. As the relationship gets serious and the lady brings up marriage, Frank is quick with his exit line: "Women fall in love when they get to know you. Men are just the opposite. When they finally know you they're ready to leave" (*D*, 38). Although "American Express" is Salter's longest story, it is a masterpiece of compression, as if Tom Wolfe's *Bonfire of the Vanities* (1987) had been distilled into 22 pages. It is indeed a story of vanity, New York life, eastern wealth, the American dream of success, and finally of time passing. The sentences of the story float wonderfully on a sea of reality: the lives of second-generation lawyers, New York social climbing, male friendship, and the triadic nature of desire. The "American Express" of the title is the fast track of material success, the crass version of the American dream. "The city was divided," Salter writes, "into those going up and those coming down, those in crowded restaurants and those on the street, those who waited and those who did not, those with three locks on the door and those rising in an elevator from a lobby with silver mirrors and walnut paneling" (*D*, 35). Frank and Alan have it all, including their final prize, Eda, the schoolgirl. Although Alan is at first shocked by Frank's suggestion they share her, once she complies, he convinces himself, "It was the most natural thing in the world," despite what he senses as her unhappiness (*D*, 52). The violation at the story's end parallels the ethical violation that had catapulted the two men to legal success. We are left with a final image of the chasm of vision between the upper and lower echelons of existence. Alan looks out his second-floor window at a delivery boy driving off on his motorbike, someone who "was part of that great, unchanging order of those who live by wages, whose world is unlit and who do not realize what is above" (*D*, 52). What is above are the unspoken possibilities.

Salter told me the story "evolved from long days spent in the trash heap of things heard, known, imagined, etc." (Letter, 1992). The acts of the story are there for the judging, but Salter has written no morality tale. His tone is imbued with sympathy, nostalgia, and respect for each character's weakness. Even minor characters are illuminated in brief paragraphs that function like side rooms, worlds in miniature, off the story's main corridor. The two principals are neither satirized nor given any comeuppance. Salter's attitude toward them, as indeed toward all the characters in his stories, is expressed in the adage of a minor character in the story, an older lawyer: "No defendant was too guilty, no case too clear-cut" (*D*, 28).

Salter's three stories about women demonstrate the range of his sympathy and should put to rest any categorization of him as a macho writer limited to a male viewpoint. Considering the strength of character of

Nedra in *Light Years* and the presence of Anne-Marie in *A Sport and a Pastime,* the opposite case could be made. "Dusk," first published as "The Fields at Dusk" in *Esquire* (August 1984), is among his best stories, with all his characteristic strengths of compression, detail, juxtaposition, and telling metaphor combining in a portrait of a 46-year-old woman who has survived losses and defeats only to be faced with one more. The following description of Mrs. Chandler, her married name and the only one we know her by, is typical of Salter's shorthand aplomb: "She was a woman who lived a certain life. She knew how to give dinner parties, take care of dogs, enter restaurants. She had her way of answering invitations, of dressing, of being herself. Incomparable habits, you might call them. She was a woman who had read books, played golf, gone to weddings, whose legs were good, who had weathered storms, a fine woman who no one now wanted" (*D*, 113). In the hands of lesser writers, such generic comments fall flat, but Salter's intonations are totally convincing, his last sentence dropping like a verdict on her fate.

Her husband gone, for another woman, and her son dead, Mrs. Chandler maintains herself as she maintains her beautiful Hamptons house, with dignity. "The house is my soul, she used to say" (*D*, 114). She has recovered from her losses enough to be functioning independently and with some complaisance and has become involved with her handyman, Bill, a man six years younger, estranged from his wife. The story's only contemporary event is Bill's visit after a noticeable absence of a month to tell her he will not be coming around any more because he and his wife have reunited. Now he hopes to secure the house (we recall its identification with her) before making his final exit. He sets about to fix a dripping pipe and check the heating in the upstairs bedroom, and it is while they are chatting in this intimate part of the house at dusk that he breaks the news about going back to his wife. She accepts his leaving with bleak resignation and without protest, but "the summer with its hope and long days was gone" (*D*, 118). Winter, which parallels the embers of the day and the winter of her soul, is around the corner. The story closes with a dazzling, inspired connection by Salter, as he describes Mrs. Chandler first looking at a mirror realizing "she would never be younger," then turning her thoughts to geese being hunted in the surrounding fields at dusk, imagining one particular bird lying in the grass, "dark sodden breast, graceful neck still extended, great wings striving to beat, bloody sounds coming from the holes in its beak. She went around and turned on lights. The rain was coming down, the sea was crashing, a comrade lay dead in the whirling darkness" (*D*, 119).

Both "Foreign Shores" (*Esquire,* September 1983) and "Twenty Minutes" (*Grand Street,* Winter 1988) are about women of a class comparable to that of Mrs. Chandler. The settings are different, one set, like "Dusk," in the Hamptons, the other out west, probably in Colorado; but the women are alike in that they are no longer married (both husbands are in California) and they are young, knowledgeable, and affluent enough to live well. Salter's empathy with these women is remarkable. In "Foreign Shores," readers meet Gloria, 29 with a 5-year-old son, Christopher, whom she has neither the time nor the inclination to mother. Hence the use of nannies, and the latest is Truus, a 19-year-old Dutch au pair without a work permit, whose appearance could use some improving. Gloria drinks and burns holes in the carpet and drives her car into ditches after nights at the local tavern, but she has a strong moral antenna when it comes to Christopher's caretakers; when she discovers letters Truus had received from a young man who worked in Saudi Arabia and whom Truus had fallen for, Gloria is scandalized by their sexually explicit nature and by the fellow's occupation as a recruiter of youth for pornography or prostitution. She fires Truus immediately and comments bitterly when she sees how hard it is for her son to say good-bye, "They always love sluts" (*D,* 71). This bit of jealousy is heightened in the story's conclusion when a couple of years later Gloria comes across a photo in *Town and Country* of a garden party in Brussels that shows a face that is almost certainly Truus. She is dizzied by the inequity of such success by classless women; it reminds her of the girl her former boyfriend Ned had decided to marry, someone "who used to work in the catering shop just off the highway near Bridgehampton" (*D,* 73). And as for Truus, "It was unbearable to think of her being invited to places, slimmer now, sitting in the brilliance of crowded restaurants with her complexion still bad beneath the makeup and the morals of a housefly. The idea that there is an unearned happiness, that certain people find their way to it, nearly made her sick" (*D,* 73).

This is one of Salter's longer stories, and it draws the reader quite thoroughly into the world of wealthy divorcées and their ideas of class as well as the world of au pairs and the impressions they make on the kids they sometimes pretend to care for. As well, the story takes us to the foreign shores of European decadence in the straightforward solicitation of Truus's Saudi-based friend: "If you came to Europe it would be great, one [letter] said. We would travel and you could help me. We could work together. I know you would be very good at it. The girls we would be looking for are between 13 and 18 years old. Also guys, a little older"

(*D*, 70). The spin that Gloria puts on all this, of course, is how the wicked do prosper; but then the story reveals more intimately that it is class and not morality that is the real issue in Gloria's set of values.

In "Twenty Minutes," Jane Vare, a skilled horsewoman who once bought a greyhound to save its life, is out riding one of her faster but less reliable horses. When he goes to jump a ditch and gate, something happens and she flies over his head and he falls on her. "She was stunned but felt unhurt. For a minute she imagined she might stand up and brush herself off" (*D*, 20). The reality, however, is that her organs have been crushed and she soon realizes "she had some time. Twenty minutes, they always said" (*D*, 21). The story is a tour de force in that it takes about 20 minutes to read and the same length of time for Jane Vare to die. In the course of that time, her mind turns from her immediate situation (encouraging the horse to return home, hoping someone would come up the dirt road, and urging herself to live up to her father's code, which demands that she at least try to save herself even if it only means crawling a few yards) to the denial of it by recapitulating the highs and lows of her life. In these spare flashbacks, Salter creates an entire life through the filter of her memories. There was the time when she had given a party for Bill Millinger and had offered herself to him after everyone had left, only to be told he was "the other way." She recalls another occasion in Saratoga when she was the one who said no to the elegant Englishman who had to have her that night or not at all. And her most painful memory is of the ride home one day when her husband casually told her he was breaking off an affair that he wrongly assumed she knew about. Eventually he left and went to Santa Barbara "and became the extra man at dinner parties" (*D*, 24). And then she summons a flurry of halcyon moments from that first apartment on Eleventh Street, to the morning in Sausalito, to the hotel in Haiti, and her announcement to her father that she was getting married. Those early days when Henry started his own landscaping business and "they had their own world . . . . like two sun-bleached children" become her last memory. She is found by a man from a nearby house and a high school girl, who have just come from making out in his pickup truck in the woods. Ironically, they passed her by earlier but were probably too distracted to notice. This final irony becomes a commentary on how the immediate urges of those in the thick of life distract them from the needs of those in dusk's shadows.

"Comet," written after *Dusk and Other Stories,* appeared in *Esquire*'s summer fiction issue of 1993. It belongs with the group of stories about men who confront the past. Philip Ardet, "mannerly and elegant," is in his third marriage, a comfortable one, with Adele, also divorced. In the course of a dinner party one evening, conversation drifts to the plight of a woman in their midst who had just discovered her husband had been having an affair for seven years. When Phil questions whether this discovery wipes out the years of happiness, Adele, who has been drinking, drops juicy revelations about Phil's previous marriages. It seems he had left his first wife and family for his son's 20-year-old tutor, who turned out to be a high-class call girl, the discovery of which did not deter him from marrying her. Exposed before the group but unchagrined, Phil is incapable of explaining to them how it was, for "none of them could visualize Mexico City and the first ecstatic year, driving down to the coast for the weekend, through Cuernavaca, her bare legs beside him with the sun lying on them, her arms, the dizziness and submission he felt with her as before a forbidden photograph, as before an overwhelming work of art. Two years in Mexico City ignoring the wreckage. It was the sense of godliness that empowered him."[3] In place of futile explanation, Phil simply affirms that, given the chance, he would do it all over again.

The story centers on two familiar themes: the priceless and ineffable glory of certain moments in life, no matter how costly, and the way relationships can deteriorate. Both ideas are carried in the final scene when Adele follows Philip outside and finds him gazing at a comet, which becomes a metaphor for the times with his second wife in Mexico City. Adele cannot see the comet, although he directs her gaze to it, and she urges him to return to the party and save the comet for tomorrow. He replies, "It won't be there tomorrow. One time only" ("Comet," 76). He remains, and the sight of her walking back to the house becomes emblematic of the stages their relationship has passed through. "She became smaller and smaller across the lawn, reaching first the aura, then the brightness, then tripping on the kitchen stairs" ("Comet," 76). Adele's glow has faded with time and her increased drinking, and the carelessness with which she exposed Phil's past to the group's scorn was as clumsy and ugly as her fall on the stairs. Finally, her walking away signals as well the end of their relationship, for it was a critical "one time only" possibility of intimacy that Philip had offered to her in the vision of the comet.

## Reviews and Assessment

Reviewers sang *Dusk*'s merits. Playwright A. R. Gurney, in the *New York Times Book Review*, exemplified the general reaction: "This is fine writing, these are first rate stories, and James Salter is an author worth more attention than he has received so far" (Gurney, 11). Gurney commented on the centrality of dusk in the stories as a metaphor of endings in relationships, lives, or whole cultures. In the *Los Angeles Times* Richard Eder marveled at the "resplendent" quality of Salter's writing, noting how "in his carefully laid gunpowder train [he] drops a white-hot phrase that ignites the whole thing, but it is as precise as a match flare."[4] Across the Atlantic in the *Times Literary Supplement,* Freddie Baveystock was equally laudatory of Salter's "timeless" and "evocative" collection, singling out "American Express" as the best story and "the purity of Salter's prose" as the book's greatest pleasure.[5] Another English voice, Anthony Quinn, raved about Salter's "superbly accomplished stories." Quinn saw "the quiet miseries that simmer between men and women" as Salter's central theme, and he appreciated both "the economy and speed with which Salter constructs a plot" and "the way Salter can stitch different narrative viewpoints into a seamless weave."[6] Michiko Kakutani, writing in the *New York Times,* found "instances where Mr. Salter's taste for symmetry results in a certain flattening-out of the ambiguities of reality," but Kakutani admitted these were rare lapses. More positively, she flagged one of Salter's constant virtues, his ability to "delineate a character in a line or two, giving us, in addition to his melancholy heroes, bright, hard cameos of the people they encounter."[7]

Two reviewers had definite qualifications about Salter's success. Richard Burgin in the *Partisan Review* complained that in some of the stories—surprisingly including "Dusk" and "Twenty Minutes," which were generally singled out for praise by other reviewers—"there's an all too knowing irony and an enervating sense of defeat before the battle's been fought."[8] And the book's harshest review, by Peter Wild in *Western American Literature,* said that Salter wasted his good writing on "hackneyed and unrevealing situations." Wild felt that for all the stories' technical merits, "we are dealing with personalities trivialized into bathos."[9]

Two reviewers agree that *Dusk* places Salter in the company of first-rate short story writers, although they pick different examples. Robert Burke claims Salter is on a par with Alice Adams and that he is better than Raymond Carver.[10] Ned Rorem says Salter "inhabits the same rarefied heights as such establishment idols as Flannery O'Connor, Paul Bowles, Tennessee Williams (whose stories are much superior to his plays) and John Cheever." Rorem's attempt to describe Salter's style in terms of music is noteworthy: "Its spell stems less from a gift to spin yarns than from rhythm and echo, from color in the guise of 'dark' vowels and clipped consonants, and from tune-like phrases with their repetition and variation—aural attributes ringing through the pages with a sensuality as continual, and as impossible to depict in words, as the continual sensuality in, say, Debussy."[11]

The accolades of most reviewers were confirmed when *Dusk* the following year earned the P.E.N./Faulkner Award. It is the highest honor yet awarded to Salter, establishing his reputation as a short story writer. Indeed, the collection as a whole is distinguished. Its five best stories are "Dusk," "The Cinema," "Twenty Minutes," "American Express," and "Dirt." What sets his short fiction apart are the subtle melodies of his prose, his ability to enter the dreams and disappointments of his characters, and his success in discovering metaphoric resonances for their fates. Short stories have no time to make up for false steps, and they must begin and end as if they were carved in stone. Salter's stories proceed with such calm inevitability. They seem as natural as the familiar front-porch swing, and as suggestive as the white lighthouse sitting serenely above the clamoring waves.

## Chapter Eight
# Memoirist *(Burning the Days)*

Autobiography may come to be seen as the literary form of the 1990s. There has been a flowering of celebrated personal accounts, from Frank McCourt's astonishing narration of his Irish boyhood in *Angela's Ashes* to Mary Karr's intimate tale of growing up in east Texas in *The Liars' Club*. College courses in autobiography, once rare, are now listed routinely in English departments across the country, exposing the variety, subtlety, and artfulness of a genre that could no longer be thought of as pedestrian and straightforward after the appearance of Vladimir Nabokov's *Speak, Memory* in 1966. Creative writing courses in "personal writing" are springing up in campuses across the country, swept along by a crest of popular demand for the form. McCourt's book, his first ever, surprised many in the publishing industry when it became a runaway bestseller with more than one million six hundred thousand copies sold.[1] The success of other personal accounts like *Drinking: A Love Story, The Kiss, The Shadow Man, Autobiography of a Face,* and Doris Kearns Goodwin's *Wait till Next Year* has sent many writers back to their cobwebbed journals and has spawned guidebooks like Judith Barrington's *Writing the Memoir* and workshops on writing about oneself. "The confessional mode," as James Wolcott notes, "is becoming formalized and institutionalized . . . as a foster child to the creative writing of fiction."[2] Why this outpouring of personal writing and why this appreciation for it? One explanation is that, as we are approach the year 2000, looking back—the whole enterprise of the memoir—may be our collective psyche's way of facing the close of a major chapter. Thus far, the fin de siècle seems not to have imposed itself on our public consciousness in any obvious way other than the apprehension that our computers are not equipped to handle the change of digits, our contemporary version of apocalypse. The phenomenon of the memoir, however, could well be our increasingly more aged population's displaced way of dealing with the anxiety of the end of a century, the death of a millennium.

*Burning the Days* (1997) may one day come to be seen as one of the most important memoirs of the century, a summation not only of its author's life but a reprise of the major chords of our time as filtered through an urbane sensibility, American in its formation and European in its cultivation. Born in 1925, Salter enjoyed his salad days right in the middle of our century. Although he graduated from West Point a year too late to see combat in the war that was the period's defining moment, his whole being was a drawn bow pointed toward that conflict. Later he would volunteer for air combat in Korea. War, heroism, love, friendship, ambition, the arts, the movies, and the literary life—these are the topics of Salter's book. His experiences are varied—child of New York, cadet, pilot, novelist, screenwriter, director, journalist, short story writer, and acquaintance of the great and the near great from these disparate worlds—providing a privileged slant on the heart of our times.

*Burning the Days* was a long time coming. Salter started it in 1986 after an autobiographical piece called "The Captain's Wife," which would become one of the chapters, had appeared in *Esquire*. This account of his Honolulu days in the Air Force, during which he fell in love with his friend and fellow officer's wife, elicited enthusiasm from his editor, Joe Fox, who urged him to continue in the same vein. With some misgivings about committing to writing at length about himself, Salter signed a contract with Random House to deliver a memoir to them by 1989, a deadline he would miss by only seven years. The personal nature of the writing was not easy for Salter, who has generally guarded his privacy over the years. "As a result," he admits, "the writing was slow. Wearied by self-revelation, I would stop for months before starting in again" (*BD*, x). Of course, writing deliberately has always been Salter's way. He does not compose according to a schedule, sitting down only when he feels he is ready to put words on paper. For this book, getting ready meant revisiting old haunts in order to conjure spirits from the past. Salter recounted in a letter to me in 1992 that he had just been to Arkansas, the scene of his first flight training. Walking up to the same desk he had approached in 1946 as a fresh young cadet, he asked the receptionist, "Remember me?"

Many of the book's chapters appeared in magazines and journals in the intervening years as Salter, who has never had the kind of book sales that induce complacency, exercised the journalistic instinct that has been one of his means of survival as a writer. When the time came to put the whole together in the form of a book, he was meticulous in shaping the various parts to make a unified impression. All this took time, and Salter was in no hurry, for he recognized the importance of the undertaking. He knew that the act of writing an autobiography could be seen as mere vanity unless the book somehow transcended the personal events it narrated. He realized the nature of the gamble and—inspired by *Speak, Memory* and Isak Dinesen's *Out of Africa*—the size of the stakes; and he recognized, given his age, that the dice would circle the table only so many more times. Each roll from here on would have to be a good one if he had any chance of having his name inscribed on the wall. Make no mistake about it, *Burning the Days* is propelled by the blazing ambition and deliberate confidence of genius. One hallmark of genius is that it always is aware of itself even when recognition by others is thin, and Salter has always believed in himself and been unambiguous about the lofty aspirations of his writing. He recounts in the memoir an incident that took place in 1954 when, still in the service and traveling by train to Frankfurt, he came across Dylan Thomas's *Under Milk Wood* for the first time: "The words dizzied me, their grandeur, their wit. . . . I had never made anything as sacred or beautiful as the poem I had read, and the longing to do so, never wholly absent, rose up in me. I gazed out the window. It was 1954, winter. Could I?" (*BD*, 231). *Burning the Days* is Salter's effort to make out of the fragments of his memories something sacred and beautiful. The book is fashioned as carefully and as resonantly as any piece of fiction.

## Paths of Glory

The story proceeds, like a river, from the feeding streams of family origins to the sea, the full expanse of the ocean that is set before the Long Island home Salter built in 1986 and will one day likely be the scene of his last good-byes. The journey flows according to life's rough chronology, with chapters about Salter's youth, his West Point days, flight training in the South, early Air Force assignments in the Pacific, aerial combat in Korea, assignments in Germany, his early writing career and friendship with Irwin Shaw, Paris days, his fling with the movies, and the writing of his major novels. It is, however, in the bends of the river's course, where the water seems to grow still in motionless pools, that its real depths appear. At such turns Salter manages to say a lot about himself without providing exhaustive detail, often relating an anecdote about someone else that exposes his own predilections. One example of this is the story about Salter's good friend and mentor, Robert Phelps. Phelps apparently never forgave his own father's betrayal of his mother and the father's enlisting his young son as a go-between. After the father left the family and married the girl with whom he'd been having the affair, Phelps said good-bye to him forever. Later when the father as an old man lay dying and friends pleaded with Phelps to go to him, he refused. Salter relates the incident without comment. Although one could not imagine him acting like Phelps, within the galvanizing resolution of such decisiveness Salter himself can be found.

Another personal revelation hinted at through the Phelps anecdote is that Salter's definition of himself came partly from opposition to his own father, who served as a cautionary example of failure in life. After graduating with a first at West Point, Salter's father did nothing of note. He brokered some successful real estate transactions in his early years as a deal maker, but after he returned from the desk job to which he had been recalled during World War II, things unraveled on the business front and he could never pull them together. When bad loans and collapsed deals occurred, his spirit was broken and he gave up. The effect on Salter was twofold, molding a determination to make a mark on life and leaving a void he would fill with other father figures. Perhaps a need to distance himself from his father may have also contributed, albeit unconsciously, to Salter's decision to change his name from the paternal Horowitz. Even as a teenage boy he had practiced for this insurrection by using the pen name of James Arnold on poems he had published in a national journal. Of course, I do not mean to imply that Salter's father had an entirely counterinfluence on him. The author fondly recalls accompanying his father on visits to Salter's grandmother, relating the devotion and care his father displayed at those times. Salter, as if in imitation, is equally attendant upon his own mother, who in her nineties still lives in her own apartment in New York, flying regularly from Colorado to visit her and talking with her frequently via telephone.

Goaded, then, by the negative example of his father's failure, Salter determined to succeed. At different times in life three distinct avenues seemed possible, although only two of them eventually proved worthy of ambition. The first was military glory. Although at West Point he initially rebelled against the rigidities that created a wrenching change of environment for the softer cultural self he had been nurturing during his prep school years, Salter came to embrace the Army ideals of duty, honor, and country, "the great virtues [which] were cut into stone above the archways and inscribed in the gold of class rings" (*BD*, 59). The war was in progress, and, like many of his classmates, Salter responded to its call for glory. He writes, "There were images of the struggle in the air on every side, the fighter pilots back from missions deep into Europe, rendezvous times still written in ink on the back of their hands, gunners with shawls of bullets over their shoulders, grinning and risky, I saw them, I saw myself, in the rattle and thunder of takeoff, the world of warm cots, cigarettes, stand-downs, everything that had mattered falling away" (BD, 67–68). What had mattered before, poetry and art and love, seemed trivial against the images of war. Death in battle seemed especially glorious. "What more," he asks, "is there to wish than to be remembered? To go on living in the narrative of others? More than anything I felt the desire to be rid of the undistinguished past, to belong to nothing and no one beyond the war" (BD, 68).

Salter graduated too late for that war, but he pursued those same ideals in volunteering for air combat in Korea and in his 12-year military career. The time, however, was not ripe for glory. Not becoming an ace in Korea was a bitter pill, for Salter always felt he had been capable of it, and others confirmed this opinion. Although he never boasts of his flying ability, clearly he was one of those naturals in the F-86 who felt "absolute control of the airplane" and could exert that control under fire (BD, 131). Later in Germany he would lead an aerial acrobatics team, but neither this nor gunnery prizes in North Africa fulfilled the proportions of his ambition, which gradually began to bend back to his earlier interests in writing and literature. When the acceptance of a novel for publication opened the gate onto another path to distinction, the time came to leave the life of soldiering. Salter was 32 and had been in uniform since he was 17. It was not an easy departure, for he had wholeheartedly embraced the military ideals and the pilot's life. Just how deeply is evident from the exalted place given in his memoir to the distinguished accomplishments of men he had flown with in Korea and elsewhere. Ed White and Buzz Aldrin are among the front ranks of Salter's heroes, the kind he had longed to be. Men who affected history. One of the book's most moving vignettes is a scene of Salter and an Italian mistress in a posh New York hotel making love in front of the television while Aldrin was on the way to the moon: "Pleasure and inconsequence on one hand, immeasurable deeds on the other" (BD, 286).

Although one senses that only immense literary accomplishments could match these "immeasurable deeds" of his military heroes, Salter transferred his deepest longings for glory to writing. From the beginning it was never just a livelihood, and indeed, considering the modest sales, it was hardly even that. Writing was another way, one of the deepest, into "the narrative of others." One of the pleasures of reading Burning the Days is feeling Salter's love for literature, not always apparent in writers, and his reverence for the saints of the literary pantheon. The litany of his favorites is long: Babel, Colette, Céline, Chekhov, Faulkner,

Fitzgerald, Genet, Gide, Maupassant, Nabokov, St.-Exupéry, Flannery O'Connor, and Marguerite Duras. And woven into the liturgy are anecdotes culled from their lives that, like those of his friends, reveal much about himself. He writes, for example, of St.-Exupéry and "his affair on one side of the world or the other, among the palms of California or the forests of East Africa, with Beryl Markham—two ecstatic souls, somehow unjealous of each other. Over the years St.-Exupéry managed to progress, for me, from being a mere figure of culture to one of enviable flesh and blood. In such footsteps I would follow" (*BD*, 77).

Of course, the writer who made the literary life seem both desirable and obtainable was Irwin Shaw, and Salter devotes nearly a chapter to this "forgotten king." He met Shaw in 1961 when the fruits of the older writer's career were all being harvested. Salter had published two undistinguished novels and brought to the table only "the arrogance of failure." The two hit it off immediately, and Shaw welcomed Salter into one of his many circles, effectively providing the ticket to the dance. Over the years, they stayed close, and when later Shaw lay dying in Switzerland, Salter flew across the Atlantic to be with him, arriving only hours late.

What Salter mostly admired about Shaw was his generosity and his lifestyle. Shaw's literary reputation, however, had already started to drop, with his best work long behind him. Salter set his sights higher. And with the publication of *A Sport and a Pastime,* he believed he had bridged that enormous gap between desire and achievement. Salter is frank in assessing his own work, some would say severe. Of his third novel, however, he writes: "It was my ambition to write something . . . [that] could not be brushed away. During its writing I felt great assurance. Everything came out as I imagined" (*BD*, 316). When Salter's own publisher failed to agree and turned the book down, and others did the same, the author was shaken. They said "the book was repetitive. Its characters were unsympathetic. Perhaps I was mistaken and in isolation had lost my bearings or failed to draw the line, emerging as a kind of hermit with skewed ideas" (*BD*, 317). Only after the book was accepted did Salter's assurance about it return.

When he finished his next book, Salter was as elated as he had been after *A Sport and a Pastime.* Like its predecessor, however, *Light Years* went begging for a publisher until Joe Fox took it at Random House. Salter recalls that when Fox called it " 'an absolutely marvelous book in every way' . . . I had the exultation of believing it" (*BD*, 332). Fox had been the editor, Salter knew, for writers whose names were revered, names like Paul Bowles, Truman Capote, Ralph Ellison, and Philip Roth. If such a ferryman liked your work, it seemed the journey to glory was nearly assured. And Salter admits, "I wanted glory" (*BD*, 332). It was not to be. With low sales and a scathing review appearing in the *New York Times Book Review*, the book labored in obscurity although it has been twice reprinted since and is still in print.

"What is it you want?" a friend's wife asked Salter one relaxed evening after dinner. When Salter hesitated, his friend, knowing him well, replied for him, "To be immortal" (*BD*, 322). Salter clearly believes his best chance for immortality rests on *Light Years* and *A Sport and a Pastime*, although he ranks some of his stories in their class. Of his fifth novel, *Solo Faces*, which some judge above or equal to the other two, he is not so fond, having felt "nothing ecstatic about the writing, as there had been in the two previous novels" (*BD*, 284). In the end, Salter has faith in the judgment of readers. At some point, he feels, a book must be popular, even if that point occurs after the writer has been buried. He will take his chances, consoled by the fact that "it is only in books that one finds perfection, only in books that it cannot be spoiled. Art, in a sense, is life brought to a standstill, rescued from time. The secret of making it is simple: discard everything that is good enough" (*BD*, 333).

In the midst of his writing *A Sport and a Pastime*, still another path to glory had offered itself. In New York, "the thrilling city" suffused in the mid-1960s with "a kind of Athenian brilliance," the new European cinema was breaking creative ground. Films by Antonioni, Truffaut, Fellini, and Godard were playing in all the festivals, "representing a new kind of film, more imaginative and penetrating than our own" (*BD*, 237). So when the opportunity came to write a film script, Salter was eager. Although his first script was never made into a movie, it did lead to Salter's meeting Robert Redford and thereafter to his first movie credit as screenwriter for *Downhill Racer*. That film's success at the box office, however, and its favorable critical reception were not enough to satisfy Salter, who saw mostly the flaws. Nor did two other films he wrote around the same time please him a great deal more, even though *Three*, which he directed as well as wrote, won recognition at Cannes. Through these experiences, untold scripts written but never made, and a final film, *Threshold*, he became convinced that this life was not a writer's life. The real glory in film, after the actors of course, belonged to directors, the burden of whose work Salter realized he was not willing to carry. Film writers were like sous-chefs, preparing all the ingredients, but the director always shaped the final dish. Some of the best scripts, in fact, never make it to table. Eventually Salter discarded any ambition he may have originally harbored for making a mark in film. He has come, in fact, to view the industry itself as something less than noble because of its impurities. Near the end of the chapter about his involvement in the glittering world of filmdom, he says movingly: "I was a *poule* for ten years, fifteen. I might easily have gone on longer. There was wreckage all around, but like the refuse piled behind restaurants I did not consider it—in front they were bowing and showing me to the table" (*BD,* 286).

## The Glories of Life and the Shadow of Death

A number of things distinguish *Burning the Days,* and it is hard to sort them out because they are interwoven. Salter's style, limpid and precise, carries the narration like a cat burglar looting an opulent apartment. He knows where everything is and is unhurried in his attention to details. Forget the banal and the worthless trinkets, Salter's prose will only shine on the valuable and the essential. Within a context that takes in most of the great events of our century—the crash of 1929, the depression, the fervor of World War II, the emergence of film and then television, and the milestones of space exploration—Salter sings, like the poet, of arms and a man. Heroism in war and art, however, is not all he celebrates within his epic. The other valuables are friendship, pleasure, and love, distinct but overlapping experiences that are featured throughout the book in scenes and stories within scenes. One thing Salter took from his screen-writing days is the ability to create an atmosphere with a few telling details and let the actors deliver their devastating lines. He does this frequently in *Burning the Days,* fading in and out of scenes of friendship, pleasure, and love.

Shaw, Lane Slate, Robert Emmett Ginna, Ben Sonnenberg, and Christopher Mankiewicz are among the portraits of friendship Salter paints. Of their attraction, Salter writes, "I like men who have known the best and the worst, whose life has been anything but a smooth trip. Storms have battered them, they have lain, sometimes for months on end, becalmed. There is a residue even if they fail. It has not been all tinkling; there have been grand chords" (*BD,* 297). He relates an anecdote of Ginna and himself flying to Europe long after the years of first-class travel were past and Ginna's credit cards had been revoked. As the plane lands, Ginna "reaches around near his feet. His shoes have disappeared. 'Anyway, *they're* in first class,' he says wryly. They had been

handmade, though now a nail was coming up through the sole of one"
(*BD*, 277).

Among Salter's pleasures are gossip, places, food and drink. He
delights in listening to and retelling scandalous stories like that told to
him in Rome of the three Italian contessas who out of boredom one
evening picked up a 13-year-old gypsy girl and brought her to the home
of a journalist friend as a gift and for their own voyeuristic amusement.
Salter casts himself in the familiar role, crystallized in many portraits by
Henry James, of the naïve American partaking in Europe of fruit from
the tree of knowledge of good and evil. At one point, in the midst of the
initiation, he remarks, "The thing I failed for a long time to understand
was the connection between the vineyards, the great houses, the clois-
ters of Europe and the corruption, the darkness, the riches. They have
been always dependent on one another, and without each other could
not exist" (*BD*, 252).

Salter lavishes the places themselves with attention, which is even
better than praise. Rome, Paris, New York, California in 1975. Of the
latter, he writes: "This was the Coast, the fabled Coast. Girls with hair
blowing and sunburned limbs. . . . Cool morning mist and the sound of
waves, cries of children in the street, the fronds plunging down from the
heights of the tree. Malibu. Dank sand beneath one's feet in the narrow
passageway that led to the beach, the vines overhead glittering with
sun. A steamer basket arrived from my new agent, Evarts Ziegler; fruit
and wine in a frock of apricot-colored cellophane. *Welcome to California,*
the card read. It was signed simply, *Ziggy*" (*BD*, 289–90). Paris, of
course, was a revelation to Salter in the early 1950s, and he has returned
to it frequently as the holy city of his secular religion. In Paris, "the
rooms were chill but they had proportion and there was more than a
hint of another life, free of familiar inhibitions, a sacred life, this great
museum and pleasure garden evolved for you alone" (*BD*, 198). Paris
was his novitiate, and to it he returns when his faith needs bolstering.

Not the least of the pleasures, of course, is love. Salter, even in his
seventies, is attractive to women. In photographs of him as a young
pilot, he cuts a dashing figure, sharp-jawed and confident. Although he
is discreet in the memoir—some would say tantalizingly vague—clearly
he has been drawn to women throughout his life. Given the importance
of sexual love in the novels, one would have been disappointed had there
been no frank revelations in this book. Indeed there are such disclosures.
Monumental among them is his love for a fellow officer's wife when they
were stationed in Honolulu. The husband became Salter's best friend at

the same time the wife and Salter were falling deliriously in love. Although the shackles of conscience and honor prevented love's consummation, Salter and Paula developed an emotional intimacy that constituted an even deeper infidelity. Perhaps it always seems so in an affair, but in this case the emotions were far-reaching, for Paula actually selected Salter's future wife for him. This, he says, was her way of leaving her mark on him. Later, after Paula and her husband had divorced, she and Salter drew close again. He does not say at what level their relationship continued, but it is not out of coyness, I believe, but rather because it is not important. What matters is Paula's impact on him and her influence on the course of his life.

Of his wife of 24 years, Ann, Salter has almost nothing to say. It would be unfair, perhaps to both of them, to speculate why. He does mention that as part of his inspiration for *Light Years* came the realization that "marriage lasted too long," and he admits, "I was perhaps thinking of my own" (*BD*, 331). Apparently, Salter did not feel bound in his marriage by the same strictures of fidelity that his friendship with Paula's husband had imposed on *that* relationship. Europe's less restrictive standards undoubtedly were an influence. As one who has written journalism pieces on the delights of younger women and the bordellos of Paris, Salter does not hide fondness for the opposite sex or his most memorable affairs in his recollection. "The great engines of this world," he writes in reference to Irwin Shaw, "do not run on faithfulness" (*BD*, 207). The memoir is remarkable, however, not in the number of his amours, but in the nuances of feeling each love elicits. Remembering the girl who had been the model of Anne-Marie in *A Sport and A Pastime*, he says, "I wanted again to lie there watching her prepare as if she were alone in the room, before the performance, as it were, putting on makeup, slipping into heels" (*BD*, 344). There was also his Italian mistress, "who would fly places to meet me," and a liaison with the stunning beauty who at the time was John Huston's mistress. Of Ilena, who had enchanted royalty, Salter writes "[I]n the riches of that smile one would never be lonely or forgotten" (*BD*, 253). Ilena's lovers were many and her openness disarming. When returning from a film festival to Salter's arms, she tells him about falling into bed with a young man whose gaze devoured her. Salter comments, "I listened with some unhappiness but not anger. They say you should not tell these things to the other person, but in this case it meant little, faithfulness was not what I expected" (*BD*, 258). What Salter did expect were times like the trip to Paris, of which he writes: "I remember the hotel and the first evening. We were at the window; I was behind her, standing close. Across the river the lights of the city glittered, as far as one could see" (*BD, 258*).

Since 1976 Salter and Kay Eldredge have been together. For years they remained unmarried, retaining instead the dialect of romance, although parenthood and long domesticity have engendered the style of marriage. Since they once timed a visit to Paris for the birth of their son, it is not surprising that they intended one day to marry there. In April of 1998 they fulfilled that intention. Salter clearly considers Kay the last great gift of his life. As a younger love, she almost perfectly fits the French rule of thumb for the proper difference in ages: "The woman's age should be one half that of the man's plus seven years."[3] As a writer herself, she is a companion intellect as well, reading Salter's work with discrimination and relish, something that was absent in his marriage. On the other hand, their energies—both being writers—are too similar, too overlapping to provide bas-relief. Sometimes, Salter sighs, he wishes Kay were occupied in any other way than writing (PI, Algonquin). Yet his contentment in their life together is palpable. It is appropriate that *Burning the Days*'s last scene is of the two of them walking outside their Bridgehampton home after New Year's midnight, Salter's arm around her.

Every memoir implicitly deals with the topic of death through its looking back at times once vibrant that are now no more than wisps of memory. Salter's is explicit in its specific references to the subject and in its predominantly elegiac tone. He relates his own close calls as a young man in the Air Force: his crash in 1945 into a house while attempting a night landing in a field; combat missions over Korea when his controls froze or the enemy bore down; and later routine landings become treacherous, as when a patina of ice covered the runway. He also relates the deaths of those who affected him most: his fellow pilots in war and peace, men like Ed White and Virgil Grissom, burned alive on the launching pad at Cape Canaveral; literary figures like Lorca and St.-Exupéry; friends like Irwin Shaw, Ben Sonnenberg, and Robert Phelps; and, of course, the members of his family, his father and daughter. The last of these naturally was the most wrenching, an event about which Salter says, "I have never been able to write the story. I reach a certain point and cannot go on. The death of kings can be recited, but not of one's child" (*BD, 267*). While such a death overshadows even one's own, in relating the other deaths Salter seems to be contemplating his own end. Often the scenes of those who have gone before are dress rehearsals, like the reported last words of a dying old gentleman, "How about one

for the road?" At the book's close, Salter directly confronts his own end:
"I know, just as in dreams, I will die, like every living thing, many of
them more noble and important, trees, lakes, great fish that have lived
for a hundred years" (*BD*, 349). He goes on to compare the deaths in
nature, which seem absorbed by herd instinct and species survival, with
our own deaths, which are caught up in our singularity, and concludes,
"We are each of us an eventual tragedy. Perhaps this is why I am in the
country, to be close to the final companions. Perhaps it is only that winter is coming on" (*BD*, 350).

Salter believes that the only balance for the individual, apart from
this final companionship, is to live in the memory of others. In this light,
his memoir is a monument to those he has loved, honoring their existence. And, like all of his books, it is a bid for his own immortality.
"Life," he says, "passes into pages if it passes into anything" (*BD*, 202).
In turning the days of his life into pages, Salter is burning them, for to
write about something, he avers, is to let go of its memory and its grip
over you. And yet, in this conflagration of the past he is also immortaliz-
ing it and his own name, which he hopes will live on in the pages to
which he has bequeathed his life.

## Reviews and Assessment

The severest criticism in the reviews of *Burning the Days* is that Salter is
too reserved in his revelation of intimate details. One reviewer likens his
method to the care used in decanting a bottle of fine old wine. Salter
must have anticipated the reaction when he subtitled the book "A Recollection," for in an interview he distinguishes recollection from memoir,
although no explanation is offered of the difference between the terms.[4]
Does a recollection reveal less of oneself than a memoir? The distinction
seems a bit specious, but in Salter's mind it appears to hinge on the issue
of selectivity, for in his preface he tries to forestall expectations of complete disclosure. He compares his life to a large house with many rooms
and the chapters of his book to the house's windows. "Certain occupants," he writes, "will be glimpsed only briefly. Visitors come and go.
At some windows you may wish to stay longer, but alas. As with any
house, all within cannot be seen" (*BD*, ix).

Reviewers were not altogether content with the tour guide's decisions. They demanded to see more rooms and more deeply into some of
the ones on display. Richard Bernstein, for example, in the *New York
Times* complained, "The man himself remains studiously enigmatic,

shrouded in privacy."[5] Bernstein is disappointed that Salter does not dis-
cuss his name change or disclose anything about his first wife, not even
her name or the fact of their divorce. Although he is "dazzled by Mr.
Salter's talent," Bernstein is "annoyed by his secretiveness." After all, he
writes, "you would not know from his memoir that his first novel, 'The
Hunters,' was made into a movie starring Robert Mitchum," a piece of
information obviously more important to Bernstein than to Salter
(Bernstein, B6).

Three other reviewers echoed Bernstein's complaint. *Time*'s John
Elson called the memoir "at once uncannily precise and irritatingly
vague," wishing that Salter had talked about his change of name and his
first wife.[6] *Kirkus* noted that Salter "seems to long to absent himself
from the narrative, perhaps to escape the pain inherent in anyone's exca-
vation of his past."[7] And A. Alvarez, in the midst of an enthusiastic
review in the *New York Review of Books,* mentions that "Salter is private
even when he is writing the story of his life. *Burning the Days,* in fact, is
extraordinary for the things he doesn't mention."[8] I suspect in autobiographical writing there will always be a tug-of-war between the reader's
desire to know more, especially juicy bits of self-exposé, and the writer's
reticence, even camouflage, about sensitive areas. Selectivity is clearly a
guiding principle of Salter's recollection. In fact, he remarked to me
after finishing the book that he had enough memories left over that he
could write another volume without even touching on the material in
*Burning the Days* (PI, Guggenheim). Not that he has any plans along
those lines. On the contrary, Salter indicated that he has had enough of
the autobiographical and intends to focus on other things, including
another novel.

But what of the issues about which Salter chose to keep silent? Since
his taciturnity about the business of his name change has irked reviewers, perhaps this is the place to address the issue. In interviews Salter
explains that the change was "for the usual reasons, practical and personal. I was writing while still in the Air Force. At that time you had to
have approval of what you were writing" (Smith, 18). Of course, the Air
Force reason made sense at the time, but it does not explain the legal
switch, nor does it explain why he felt the urge to use a pen name for the
poetry he wrote in his teens.

It is true that Salter does not address the issue directly in *Burning the
Days,* but a hallmark of the book is its subtlety; and if one looks carefully, there are clues. Since the memoir is framed with the artifice of a
novel, it is appropriate to interpret its passages with imaginative dis-

cernment. The first clue is Salter's statement that a name "is the first of all poems. Even after death it keeps its power; even half-buried in newsprint or dirt, something catches the eye" (*BD*, 136). He goes on to list some names that cast spells: Paavo Nurmi, Jean Genet, Lamont Pry, Adrian Arcaud, Zane Amell. It is not hard to see that "James Salter" marches to the cadence of this list better than "James Horowitz." From his youth Salter was a poet, relishing the intonations and connotations of words. Although the genealogy of Horowitz leads back to an original meaning of hill or mountain, the closest English association is the unpleasant "horror." "Horowitz" is also harsher in sound than "Salter," which with its sibilant and labial is easy on the tongue. As for associations, "Salter" immediately suggests "salt" as in "the salt of the earth" or that which gives spice to life. Even more interesting is the homonym "Psalter," which is the book of Psalms or by extension any collection of sacred songs for devotional purposes, most appropriate for a writer like Salter whose prose limns life's daily mysteries. When I asked Salter how he picked his name, he said that he only remembered having a list and one day simply saying, "That's it" (PI, Algonquin). Is it any surprise that one who deals in words would be sensitive to the overtones of a word to which he is intimately and permanently attached? This esthetic motivation seems to me rather obvious, and perhaps that is why Salter has not acknowledged it.

The second clue is Salter's statement "A name is a destiny" (*BD*, 136). I hinted at my interpretation of this earlier in the chapter when discussing Salter's relationship with his father. It is possible that, in rejecting the example of his father's defeatism and despair, Salter also rejected the patronymic name. Salter and his father, as is clear from the memoir, were never particularly close, and the son's act of following his father's footsteps to West Point was as far as his filial responsibilities would go. At that time, although there had been setbacks to his father's dreams of success, he retained an inner flame and the flair for which Salter admired him. When after the war that flame was extinguished and he gave up, Salter's admiration turned into pity. If "a name is a destiny," then it was important for Salter to avoid the fate of his unhappy father by abandoning the destiny of his father's name.

The third clue from the memoir is Salter's account of listening on the radio as a boy to the "fervent anti-Semitic priest who broadcast every Sunday, Father Coughlin. His repeated fierce phrases beat against me" (*BD*, 4). Later at West Point Salter mentions that he abandoned going to Jewish services on Friday nights in favor of Sunday chapel, motivated it seems by the desire to fit in more completely with the life there. Alvarez alone notes this motivation in his review, saying, "Being a Jew called Horowitz can't have made his difficult life any easier, though he doesn't mention it because Jewishness was not something he had been brought up to think important. His family was nonreligious, more or less assimilated and long established in America" (Alvarez, 37). In a letter responding appreciatively but with corrections to Alvarez's review, Salter admits the notoriety his name brought, although of anti-Semitism at West Point he says, "I suppose there was some but very little in my own experience."[9]

I suspect it was less his concerns about anti-Semitism that led Salter to jettison "Horowitz" than the expectations of Semitism that the name raised, particularly for a writer. He did not need the burden of writing about ethnic experiences that were not particularly his own. As he comments in the letter to Alvarez, "The really Great Jews, Singer, Bellow, Malamud, Mailer, Roth, and in their wake many lesser, Heller, Potok, Levin, Brodkey had overwhelmed American literature, and I didn't belong, in any sense, among them. It wasn't my category." Of course, there are countless precedents among twentieth-century writers for such a change of name: Nathanael West, André Maurois, and Joseph Conrad, to name only a few. Had not Salter's own friend and substitute father figure, Irwin Shaw, been born Shamforoff? And had not the change helped Shaw deflect expectations of what a Jewish writer should write about? Salter clearly also wanted to avoid such expectations. I can understand the reviewers' curiosity about this topic, but I am surprised at their insistence that Salter address it with a literalness that would be out of keeping with the memoir's subtlety.

Two reviews overlooked the issue of Salter's reticence in their enthusiasm for *Burning the Days*. Writing in the *New York Times Book Review*, Samuel Hynes praised Salter for composing "a book of memorable stories" and for his "eloquent witness to the writer's faith in the craft he practices" (Hynes, 9). Because he interprets the book as a collection of stories with a unified narrator, Hynes has no qualification about Salter's nondisclosures. If anything, Hynes is impressed by Salter's "affairs with life" and the author's revelation of his two great avocations, "the desire for the intimate company of women" and "the desire to write not merely good prose, but the best prose, so perfectly made that it will survive the ends of life's affairs and the erosions of time" (Hynes, 9). Hynes can imagine nothing more difficult for a writer than to live with such a goal. Robert Taylor in the *Boston Globe* also was enthusiastic about Salter's memoir, admiring its "burnished splendor that belongs right up there on the shelf with Nabokov's 'Speak, Memory.' "[10] Taylor keys his reading of the book off an anecdote about Joe DiMaggio that Salter recounts as Irwin Shaw's story: "On their honeymoon Marilyn Monroe had gone off on a USO tour and came back and said, Joe, there were a hundred thousand people there and they were all cheering and clapping; you've never seen anything like it. Yes, I have, DiMaggio said. *Yes, I have!* It was Irwin's favorite story. *Yes, I have.* Three words, and you cried" (*BD*, 213). What is so distinctive about Salter's memoir according to Taylor is this "central theme of male honor [that] does not celebrate the macho swagger of the tough guy, but a DiMaggio-like pride in living up to one's ideals" (Taylor, C3).

Although the reviews of *Burning the Days* were quite positive, whether Salter will appeal to a wide readership, something that has thus far eluded him, remains to be seen. On the book's merits, Random House's confidence in bringing out such a large first edition appears well founded. Salter, however, has been there before. While he would like nothing better than a best-seller to chase away his reputation as an esoteric writer, he knows there is no predicting popularity. Even if he could, it would not alter the course of his writing, for he is an artist to his bones, committed to the task of capturing the ebb and flow of life in words. His DiMaggio-like pride in living up to his ideals, alluded to by Taylor, and his faith in the ultimate power of his art, alluded to by Hynes, lead him to look past immediate popularity and toward a more lasting glory. *Burning the Days* is eloquent testimony of that pride and that faith.

# Chapter Nine
# A Coda

Nobody would undertake the writing of a book about an author whose works he did not admire. Attention, after all, is the sincerest form of praise. And I am sure that everyone who begins a critical study such as this one sets out with sincere admiration for his subject. In the process of the writing, however, one's admiration is tried by enforced familiarity with texts one has read again and again. It is one thing to take a short trip with someone, but an ocean voyage in adjoining cabins, that's something else. It is then that one learns just how good a companion the admired author is.

I had not intended to write anything in conclusion because it seemed each of my chapters has had its own conclusion. But I would be remiss if I did not report that Salter has traveled very well indeed on this voyage. Familiarity has bred only more delight in the company of his books. I posed myself a test, which I suggest to anyone finishing such a project, to measure such delight. What would I feel if my subject had a new book coming out within the next year? Other than the deflating realization that my critique had become less than au courant, I can honestly say I would be thrilled.

Salter's is a rare talent even among accomplished writers. I can think of no other living writer whose prose has a greater density or more polish while still serving the larger ends of story. I read and reread his work searching for the mysterious thread that would bind it all together. And through all the readings, his texts retained their power to wound. His stories in the manner of all great literature are heartbreaking, not only because they are sad with the inevitable sadness of life but because that sadness is so intimately bound up with exultation in life's sharpest joys. Put simply, and this is the thread, Salter captures in prose the fading glory of life.

His greatness lies not merely in style, however, but in his ability to enter fully into diverse worlds—the defining moments of aerial combat in *The Hunters,* the back roads of rural France and young love in *A Sport and a Pastime,* the boundless days of family life in *Light Years,* and the lonely challenge of the mountain heights in *Solo Faces.* He draws us into these worlds and their characters so completely that we must measure our own lives against their glories and defeats.

As for Salter's reputation, I have no doubt that it will grow, later if not now. His stature rests on an indelible novel (*A Sport and a Pastime*), a haunting novel (*Light Years*), and a novel deeply resonant with the American tradition (*Solo Faces*). It is enhanced by two stories that are classics ("American Express" and "Dusk") and a handful of others that are very good. His memoir is the sleeper, for, if it is overlooked in the contemporary rage for lurid exposé, one day it will be unearthed like the statue of Ozymandias, a monument of a bygone time:

> a shattered visage . . . whose frown,
> And wrinkled lip, and sneer of cold command,
> Tell that its sculptor well those passions read,
> Which yet survive, stamped on these lifeless things,
> The hand that mocked them, and the heart that fed.

# Notes and References

*Preface*

    1. William Dean Howells, "Novel-Writing and Novel Reading," *Howells and James: A Double Billing,* ed. William Gibson (New York: New York Public Library, 1958), 17.

    2. W. B. Yeats, "Sailing to Byzantium," *The Collected Poems of W. B. Yeats* (New York: Macmillan, 1956), 192.

    3. Joseph Barbato, "Breaking Out," *Publishers Weekly,* 31 May 1985, 30–33.

    4. Editorial Note, *Esquire,* August 1984, 101; hereafter cited in the text.

    5. Reynolds Price, "Famous First Words: Well Begun Is Half Done," *New York Times Book Review,* 2 June 1985, 3; hereafter cited in the text.

    6. Saul Bellow, letter to James Salter, 5 August 1975.

    7. Joy Williams, letter to James Salter, 21 June 1975.

    8. A. R. Gurney, "Those Going Up and Those Coming Down," *New York Times Book Review,* 21 February 1988, 9, 11; hereafter cited in the text.

    9. Mavis Gallant, letter to Joseph Fox, 21 February 1975.

    10. James Wolcott, "Mixed Media: A Scorecard for the All-American Literary All-Star Game," *Vanity Fair,* June 1985,16.

    11. Susan Sontag, Dust Jacket, *Burning the Days* (New York: Random House, 1997).

    12. Margaret Winchell Miller, "Glimpses of a Secular Holy Land: The Novels of James Salter," *Hollins Critic* 19.1 (1982): 1–13; hereafter cited in the text.

    13. William Dowie, "*Solo Faces:* American Tradition and the Individual Talent," *Essays on the Literature of Mountaineering,* ed. Armand E. Singer (Morgantown: West Virginia University Press, 1982), 118–27.

    14. William Dowie, "James Salter: A Final Glory," *College English,* January 1988, 74–88.

    15. James Salter, "The Cinema," *Dusk and Other Stories* (San Francisco: North Point Press, 1988), 80; hereafter *Dusk* will be cited in the text as *D.*

    16. Samuel Hynes, *New York Times Book Review,* 7 September 1997, 9; hereafter cited in the text.

    17. James Salter, *Light Years* (New York: Random House, 1975; New York: Vintage, 1995), 161; hereafter cited in the text as *LY.*

    18. James Salter, *Burning the Days* (New York: Random House, 1997), 210; hereafter cited in the text as *BD.*

19. James Salter, "The Art of Fiction: CXXXIII," Interview with Edward Hirsch, *Paris Review,* Summer 1993, 91; hereafter cited in the text as "Art."

20. Linda Wagner-Martin, "Hemingway, Fitzgerald, and Stein," *Columbia Literary History of the United States,* ed. Emory Elliott (New York: Columbia University Press, 1988), 876; hereafter cited in the text.

*Chapter One*

1. James Salter, letter to the author, 11 November 1983.

2. Personal interview, Guggenheim Museum, New York, 8 January 1997; hereafter cited in the text as PI, Guggenheim.

3. James Salter, letter to the author, undated, 1992; hereafter cited in the text as Letter, 1992.

4. James Salter, "Infamy and Memory," *The New York Times* ,7 December 1991, 23L; hereafter cited in the text as "Infamy."

5. James Salter, "Europe," *Esquire,* December 1990, 114.

6. James Salter, letter to the author, 24 September 1987.

7. Personal interview, Algonquin Hotel, New York, 9 January 1997; hereafter cited in the text as PI, Algonquin.

*Chapter Two*

1. James Salter, "Ike the Unlikely," *Esquire,* December 1983, 562.

2. James Salter, *The Hunters* (New York: Harper, 1956; Washington, D.C.: Counterpoint, 1997), 37; hereafter cited in the text as *H*.

3. I have decided to use the revised edition in this chapter because it is more available than the original, which is difficult to find. Hence I will use "Connell" instead of "Saville."

4. In the original edition, DeLeo's name is Corona.

5. Elizabeth Benedict, *The Joy of Writing Sex* (Cincinnati: Story Press, 1996), 7.

6. This quotation is only in the original edition (141). In his revision Salter has excised most of the flowery language of the original, striving for greater factualness and greater purity. In seeking here to mute his rhetoric, however, Salter has cut too deeply, truncating aspects of Cleve's expectations of his relationship with Eico that seem important to the character's motivation.

7. George Barrett, *New York Times,* 4 March 1956, 36.

8. Taliaferro Boatwright, *New York Herald Tribune Book Review,* 11 March 1956, 2.

9. S. P. Mansten, *Saturday Review,* 3 March 1956, 17.

10. James Salter, *The Arm of Flesh* (New York: Harper, 1961), 15; hereafter cited in the text as *AF*.

11. *Kirkus,* 15 December 1960, 1039.

12.  Taliaferro Boatwright, *New York Herald Tribune Book Review*, 23 April 1961, 29; hereafter cited in the text.

13.  Ronald Bryden, *Spectator*, 12 January 1962, 48.

14.  *Booklist*, 1 May 1961, 547.

*Chapter Three*

1.  Pauline Kael, *Deeper Into Movies* (Boston: Atlantic Monthly Press, 1973), 46.

2.  John Huston, *An Open Book* (New York: Knopf, 1980), 5.

3.  Sidney Lumet, *Making Movies* (New York: Vintage, 1995), 8–9.

4.  Michael Shnayerson, *Irwin Shaw* (New York: Putnam's, 1989), 271–82; hereafter cited in the text.

*Chapter Four*

1.  James Salter, "Introduction," *A Sport and a Pastime* (New York: Random House, 1967); (New York: Modern Library, 1995), ix; hereafter cited in the text as *SP*.

2.  "Bookmarks," *Prairie Schooner*, Winter 1967, 448; hereafter cited in the text.

3.  T. S. Eliot, "The Love Song of J. Alfred Prufrock," *Collected Poems: 1909–1962* (Franklin Center, Penn.: Franklin Library, 1978), 3, 4, 6.

4.  Stanley Kauffmann, *New Republic*, 25 March 1967, 24; hereafter cited in the text.

5.  René Girard, *Deceit, Desire and the Novel*, trans. Yvonne Freccero (Baltimore, Md.: John Hopkins University Press, 1965), 14; hereafter cited in the text.

6.  John Irving, *A Son of the Circus* (New York: Random House, 1994), 191.

7.  Eliot Fremont-Smith, *New York Times*, 3 March 1967, L43.

8.  *Library Journal*, 15 February 1967, 798.

9.  *Time*, 14 April 1967, 122; hereafter cited in the text.

10.  Webster Schott, *New York Times Book Review*, 2 April 1967, 47.

11.  Anatole Broyard, *New York Times*, 25 June 1975, 41; hereafter cited in the text.

12.  "Book World," *The Washington Post*, 10 November 1985, 12.

13.  Elizabeth Benedict, *Los Angeles Times*, 23 March 1985, 8.

*Chapter Five*

1.  Richard Poirier, *A World Elsewhere: The Place of Style in American Literature* (London: Oxford University Press, 1966), 5; hereafter cited in the text.

2.  Susan Sontag, *Against Interpretation* (New York: Dell, 1966), 35.

3.  Robert Towers, *New York Times Book Review*, 27 July 1975, 6–7; hereafter cited in the text.

    4.  Elizabeth Benedict, *The Philadelphia Inquirer,* 2 February 1986, 143; hereafter cited in the text.
    5.  Lee Grove, *The Real Paper,* 3 December 1975, 4.
    6.  Ronald De Feo, *Saturday Review,* 9 August 1975, 41.
    7.  John Mellors, *The Listener,* 20 May 1976, 654.
    8.  Barbara A. Bannon, *Publishers Weekly,* 19 May 1975, 170.
    9.  James Wolcott, *Esquire,* July 1982, 120.
    10. Duncan Fallowell, *Spectator,* 8 May 1976, 23.
    11. Sven Birkerts, *The Nation,* 19 June 1982, 755, 757; hereafter cited in the text.

*Chapter Six*

    1.  James Salter, "Victory or Death," *Esquire,* May 1985, 195–97; hereafter cited in the text as "Victory."
    2.  George Pokorny, "Fiction in Mountaineering Literature," *Climbing,* January–February 1979, 31.
    3.  John Sheard, *Mountain,* July–August 1980, 50.
    4.  James Salter, *Solo Faces* (Boston: Little, Brown, 1979), 89–90; hereafter cited in the text as *SF.*
    5.  *SF,* 132. The original edition has a misprint in these lines. It reads: "here is a manhood that can never be taken away." Salter informed me of this in a letter dated 6 June 1983.
    6.  A. E. Housman, "To an Athlete Dying Young," *The Collected Poems of A. E. Housman* (New York: Holt, Rinehart and Winston, 1965), 32.
    7.  Charles Gaines, *Dangler* (New York: Simon & Schuster, 1980), 134; hereafter cited in the text as Gaines.
    8.  Mircea Eliade, *The Sacred and the Profane* (New York: Harcourt, 1959), 183–84.
    9.  Peter S. Prescott, *Newsweek,* 9 July 1979, 72.
    10. Peter Wolfe, *Saturday Review,* 1 September 1979, 47.
    11. Vance Bourjaily, *The New York Times Book Review,* 5 August 1979, 11; hereafter cited in the text.
    12. Francis King, *The Spectator,* 16 February 1980, 22; hereafter cited in the text.

*Chapter Seven*

    1.  James Salter, "Isaac Babel and his Daughter," *Paris Review,* Winter 1995, 157.
    2.  James Salter, letter to the author, 11 August 1986.
    3.  James Salter, "Comet," *Esquire,* July 1993, 76.
    4.  Richard Eder, *Los Angeles Times,* 17 February 1988, 4.
    5.  Freddie Baveystock, *The Times Literary Supplement,* 25 May 1990, 558.
    6.  Anthony Quinn, *The Listener,* 17 May 1990, 22.

7. Michiko Kakutani, *The New York Times*, 13 February 1988, 16.
8. Richard Burgin, *Partisan Review* 57, no. 1 (1990): 160.
9. Peter Wild, *Western American Literature*, Winter 1989, 375.
10. Robert Burke, *The Bloomsbury Review*, May–June 1988, 3.
11. Ned Rorem, "Book World," *The Washington Post*, 6 March 1988, 1.

*Chapter Eight*

1. Ken Auletta, "The Impossible Business," *The New Yorker*, 6 October 1997, 55.
2. James Wolcott, "Me, Myself, and I," *Vanity Fair*, October 1997, 212.
3. James Salter, "Younger Women," *Esquire*, March 1992, 95.
4. Dinitia Smith, "A Fighter Pilot Who Aimed for Novels but Lives on Film," *The New York Times*, 30 August 1997, NE 17–18; hereafter cited in the text.
5. Richard Bernstein, *The New York Times*, 25 August 1997, NE B6; hereafter cited in the text.
6. John Elson, *Time*, 15 September 1997, 110.
7. *Kirkus*, 1 July 1997, on-line review.
8. A. Alvarez, *New York Review of Books*, 15 January 1988, 37; hereafter cited in the text.
9. James Salter, letter to A. Alvarez, 28 January 1988.
10. Robert Taylor, *The Boston Globe*, 17 September 1997, C3; hereafter cited in the text.

# Selected Bibliography

## PRIMARY SOURCES

*Novels*

*The Arm of Flesh.* New York: Harper, 1961.
————. London: Cassell, 1962.
*The Hunters.* New York: Harper, 1956.
————. London: Heinemann, 1957.
————. London: Pan, 1958 [abridged edition].
————. Washington, D.C.: Counterpoint, 1997 [revised edition].
*Light Years.* New York: Random House, 1975.
————. London: Bodley Head, 1976.
————. San Francisco: North Point, 1982.
————. New York: Vintage, 1995.
*Solo Faces.* Boston: Little, Brown, 1979.
————. London: Collins, 1980.
————. New York: Penguin, 1980.
————. San Francisco: North Point, 1988.
*A Sport and a Pastime.* Garden City, N.Y.: Doubleday, 1967.
————. Harmondsworth, U.K., & New York: Penguin, 1980.
————. San Francisco: North Point, 1985.
————. New York: Modern Library, 1995.

*Short Story Collections*

*Dusk and Other Stories.* San Francisco: North Point, 1988.
————. London: Cape, 1990.

*Nonfiction*

*Burning the Days.* New York: Random House, 1997.

*Contributions to Books*

Introduction. *Between Meals: An Appetite for Paris* by A. J. Liebling. San Francisco: North Point, 1986; New York: Modern Library, 1995.

*Short Stories—Uncollected*

"A Cautionary Tailor." *Gentlemen's Quarterly* 58 (October 1988): 392.

"Comet." *Esquire* 120 ( July 1993): 75 –76.
"My Lord You." *Esquire* 122 (September 1994): 150 –156.

*Films*

*The Appointment.* 1969. MGM [screenwriter].
*Downhill Racer.* 1968. Paramount [screenwriter].
*Three.* 1969. United Artists [screenwriter and director].
*Threshold.* 1983. Twentieth Century-Fox [screenwriter].

## SECONDARY SOURCES

*Interviews*

Burke, Robert. "Interview with James Salter." *Bloomsbury Review* 8 (May-June
    1988): 3, 6, 18.
Hirsch, Edward. "James Salter: The Art of Fiction: CXXXIII." *Paris Review* 127
    (Summer 1993): 54 –100.
Smith, Dinitia. "A Fighter Pilot Who Aimed for Novels but Lives on Film."
    *New York Times* (25 August 1997): New England edition, 17 –18.

*Biographical*

Begley, Adam. "A Few Well-Chosen Words." *New York Times Magazine* (28
    October 1990): 40 –43, 80 –85.
Dowie, William. "James Salter." *American Short Story Writers Since World War II.*
    Vol. 130, *Dictionary of Literary Biography,* ed. Patrick Meanor, 282–87.
    Detroit: Gale Research Co., 1993.

*Critical*

Dowie, William. "A Final Glory: The Novels of James Salter." *College English* 50
    ( January 1988): 74 –88. This article affirms that each of Salter's novels
    plays a different variation on the theme of the desire for glory in the face
    of death. It describes the elemental quality of Salter's style and suggests
    that his achievement is greater than has been recognized by either the
    public or the academy.
————. "Solo Faces: American Tradition and the Individual Talent." In
    *Essays on the Literature of Mountaineering,* ed. Armand E. Singer. Mor-
    gantown: West Virginia University Press, 1982: 118 –27. This situates
    the novel within the context of mountain writing, then explains why it
    transcends that genre and is worthy of placement within the larger
    American tradition. Chapter 6 is a revised and expanded form of this
    essay.

Miller, Margaret Winchell. "Glimpses of a Secular Holy Land: The Novels of
    James Salter." *Hollins Critic* 19, no. 1 (1982): 1–13. Winchell identifies
    as a unifying motif of Salter's novels his creation of a secular paradise out
    of life's holy and imperfect moments. In introducing Salter to the acade-
    mic community, she notes "his two most compelling gifts: a poet's ear for
    lyricism, and an obsession . . . with the power of desire."

# Index

Adams, Alice, stories compared to Salter's, 108
Aimee, Anouk, 37, 38
Albee, Edward, 38
Aldrin, Buzz, 24, 114
Altemus, Ann, 8, 119
Alvarez, A., review of *Burning the Days*, 122, 124
Anderson, Sherwood, xv
Antonioni, 116; *Red Desert, The*, 37

Babel, Isaac, xv, 8, 95
Bannon, Barbara A., review of *Light Years*, 75
Barbato, Joseph, ix
Barrett, George, review of *The Hunters*, 22–23
Barrington, Judith, *Writing the Memoir*, 110
Basso, Hamilton, xiii
Baveystock, Freddie, review of *Dusk and Other Stories*, 108
Beck, Julian, 5
Beckman, Max, 1, 2
Bellow, Saul, ix, x–xi
Benedict, Elizabeth: *Joy of Writing Sex, The*, 19; review of *Light Years*, 75; review of *A Sport and a Pastime*, 59
Bergman, Ingrid, 41
Bernstein, Richard, review of *Burning the Days*, 121–22
Berryman, John, xiv
Birkerts, Sven, 75–76
Bloom, Harold, *The Western Canon*, xii
Boatwright, Taliaferro: review of *The Arm of Flesh*, 29; review of *The Hunters*, 23
Bolt, Robert, 41; *Man for All Seasons, A*, 52
Bonnard, Pierre, "The Breakfast Room," 66
Bourjaily, Vance, x; review of *Solo Faces*, 92
breakout phenomenon, ix–x
Britt, May, 32

Broyard, Anatole: review of *Light Years*, 74; review of *A Sport and a Pastime*, 59
Bryden, Ronald, review of *The Arm of Flesh*, 29
Burgin, Richard, review of *Dusk and Other Stories*, 108
Burke, Robert, review of *Dusk and Other Stories*, 108

Camus, Albert, xv
Capote, Truman, 45–46; *In Cold Blood*, 45
*Carolina Quarterly*, Salter's "Cowboy" (later retitled "Dirt") in, 94, 100
Carroll, Madeleine, 38
Carver, Raymond, stories compared to Salter's, 108; and Tom Jenks, *American Short Story Masterpieces* (editors), 101
Céline, Louis-Ferdinand, 8, 95
Chandler, Raymond, 1
Cheever, John, 8, 44; stories compared to Salter's, 108; "The Swimmer," 101
Chekhov, Anton, 95
Clark, Eleanor, 38
Colette, Sidonie-Gabrielle, 95
*Columbia History of the American Novel, The*, xii
Cooper, James Fenimore, 80
Corelli, Marie, ix, xiii
Coughlin, Father, 123
Counterpoint, 13

Davis, Stuart, 33
De Feo, Ronald, review of *Light Years*, 75
de Montherlant, Henry, 8, 95
Dickinson, Emily, 87
DiMaggio, Joe, 125
Dinesen, Isak, *Out of Africa*, 112
Di Palma, Carlo, 37
Doubleday, 45
Doubleday, Frank, 45
Dowie, William, xi–xii
Dreiser, Theodore: "Second Choice, The," 55; *Sister Carrie*, 45

137

# *The Author*

William J. Dowie Jr. grew up in New Orleans's Irish Channel, educated in those early years by the Sisters of Mercy and shaped by the small world of Annunciation Square. He went to Jesuit High School, then to Spring Hill College in Mobile, Alabama. He attended graduate school at Brandeis University on a Woodrow Wilson Fellowship and received his Ph.D. in English in 1970. He currently teaches at Southeastern Louisiana University, where he is Professor of English and Director of Graduate Studies in English.

Dowie is the author of *Peter Matthiessen* (Twayne, 1991). His essays on modern literature have been published in *Novel: A Forum on Fiction, The Heythrop Journal, College English, Louisiana Literature,* and *Aethlon: The Journal of Sport Literature.* He has contributed articles on Walker Percy to *The Art of Walker Percy,* edited by Panthea Broughton (Louisiana State University Press, 1979), and *Critical Essays on Walker Percy,* edited by J. Donald Crowley and Sue M. Crowley (G.K. Hall, 1989), and a piece on James Salter to *Essays on the Literature of Mountaineering,* edited by Armand Singer (West Virginia University Press, 1981). He has contributed entries on James Salter and Peter Matthiessen to volumes 130 and 173, respectively, of the *Dictionary of Literary Biography.*

# The Editor

Frank Day is a professor of English and head of the English Department at Clemson University. He is the author of *Sir William Empson: An Annotated Bibliography* (1984) and *Arthur Koestler: A Guide to Research* (1985). He was a Fulbright lecturer in American literature in Romania (1980–1981) and in Bangladesh (1986–1987).